Joseph Ritson, Thomas Chestre, Libeaus Launfal

Launfal

An Ancient Metrical Romance

Joseph Ritson, Thomas Chestre, Libeaus Launfal

Launfal
An Ancient Metrical Romance

ISBN/EAN: 9783744691949

Printed in Europe, USA, Canada, Australia, Japan

Cover: Foto ©Thomas Meinert / pixelio.de

More available books at **www.hansebooks.com**

Launfal,

AN ANCIENT METRICAL ROMANCE.

BY

THOMAS CHESTRE;

TO WHICH IS APPENDED THE STILL OLDER ROMANCE OF

Lybeaus Disconus.

EDITED BY

JOSEPH RITSON.

EDINBURGH:
E. & G. GOLDSMID.
1891.

LAUNFAL.

BY THOMAS CHESTRE.

THE only ancient copy of this excellent romance, known to be now extant, is contained in a manuscript of the Cotton-library, (Caligula A. II.) written, it would seem, in or about the reign ot Henry VI. in which the translator is, by Tanner, who, most absurdly, styles him "*unus regis Arthuri equitum rotundæ tabulæ,*" supposed to have lived. Two copies are preserved, in our own libraries, of the French original, by Marie de France, a Norman poetess of the thirteenth century; one in the Harleian MS. Num. 978, and the other in the Cotton, Vespasian B. XIV. The latter begins,

"*Laventure de un lay;*"

the former (being a collection of such pieces)

"*Laventure dun autre lai.*"

The English poem, which, by the way, is much enlarged, containing a surplus of near three hundred lines, appears to have been printed under the name of "Sir Lambwell;" being licensed, in the register of the Stationers-Company, to John Kynge,* in 1558, and expressly mentioned in Laneham's "Letter, whearin part cf the entertainment unto the queenz majesty at Killingworth castl, 1575, iz signified."

M. Le Grand has given the extract of a *Lai de Gruélan,* ot which, he observes, the subject is precisely the same with that of *Lanval;* though the details are altogether different. See *Fabliaux, ou contes,* A, 92.

---

* He dwelt in Creed Lane, and kept a shop at the sign of the Swan in St. Paul's Churchyard. He probably died in 1561.—JOHNSON's TYPOGRAPHIA, vol. i., p. 557.

LAUNFAL.

PART I.

Be doughty Artours dawes,[*]
That held Engelond yn good lawes,
   Ther fell a wondyr cas,
Of a ley that was ysette,[†]
That hyght Launval, and hatte yette ;[‡]
   Now herkeneth how hyt was.
Doughty Artour som whyle
Sojournede yn Kardeuyle,[§]
   Wyth joye and greet solas ;

---

[*] Dr Percy, by mistake, gives it (from Ames ?)
           "*Le* douzty Artours dawes ;"
and says that it is in his folio MS. p. 60, beginning thus—
           "Doughty in King Arthures dayes."

[†] A lay (supposed to come from the barbarous Latin *leudus*, which occurs in the epistle of Fortunatus to Gregory of Tours—
       "*Barbaros leudos harpa relidebat*,")
was what is now called a song or ballad, but generally of the elegiac kind, tender and pathetic (in French *lai*, in German *lied*, in Saxon *leod*), which was usually sung to the harp ; and of which many instances may be found in the prose *Ronnan de Tristan*, 1488, and elsewhere. See more of these ancient British lays in a note to Emare.

[‡] Thus Mary—
       "*Laventure dun autre lai*
       Cum ele avient vus cunterai,
       Fait fu dun mut gentil vassal
       En Bretans lapelent Lanval."

[§] Thus in the MS. and Mr Ellis's edition ; but read, as afterward, Kardevyle. It is Carlisle in Cumberland, where King Arthur is fabled to have had a palace and occasional residence. "On this ryver," says Froisart, mistaking the Tyne for the Esk, "standeth the towne and castell of Carlyel, the whiche some tyme was kyng Arthurs, and helde his courte there often-tymes." (English translation, 1525, fo. vii, b.) Thus, also, in an ancient Scottish romance, furtively printed by Pinkerton :—
      "In the tyme of Arthur an aunter bytydde,
        By the Turne-Wathelan, as the boke telles,
        When he to Carlele was comen and conquerour kydde," &c.
Two old ballads, upon the subject of King Arthur, printed in the "Reliques of ancient

And knyghtes that wer profitable,   10
With Artour of the rounde table,
Never noon better ther nas.
Sere Persevall,* and syr Gawayn,
Syr Gyheryes, and syr Agrafrayn, †
And Launcelot‡ Dulake,
Syr Kay, and syr Ewayn,
That well couthe fyghte yn plain,
Bateles for to take.

English Poetry." suppose his residence at *Carleile;* and one of them, in particular, says,

"At Tearne-Wadling, his castle stands."

"Tearne-Wadling," according to the ingenious editor (and which, as he observes, is evidently the Turne-Wathelan of the Scottish poem), "is the name of a small lake near Hesketh, in Cumberland, on the road from Penrith to Carlisle. There is a tradition," he adds, "that an old castle once stood near the lake, the remains of which were not long since visible:" Tearn, in the dialect of that country, signifying a small lake, and being still in use. The tradition is that either the castle or a great city, was swallowed up by the lake, and may be still seen, under favorable circumstances, at its bottom.

It is *Kardoel* in the original, and elsewhere *Cardueil.* The old romance of *Merlin* calls it "*la ville de* Cardueil *en* Galles."

* Sir Perceval le Galois, or Percival de Gales, was one of the knights of the round table. His adventures form the subject of a French metrical romance, composed, in the twelfth century, by Chrestien de Troyes, or, according to others, by a certain Manecier, Mennesier, or Menessier, and of an English one, in the fifteenth, by Robert de Thornton. The former, extant in the national library of France, and in that of Berne, is said to contain no less than 60,000 verses; a number, however, which has been reduced by others to 20,000, and even to 8,700 and 4,500. It appeared in prose at Paris, 1530, 8vo. The latter is in the library of Lincoln Cathedral.

† Gaheris (*Gueherries,* or *Guereschcs*), and Agravaine, surnamed *le orgueilleux,* were brothers to Sir Gawain, and both knights of the round table.

‡ This hero was the son of Ban, king of Benock, in the marches of Gaul and Little-Britain, and a knight-companion of the round table. He is equally remarkable for his gallantry and good fortune; being never overcome, in either joust or tournament, unless by enchantment or treachery; and being in high favour with the queen, whom he loved with singular fidelity to the last; doing for her many magnanimous deeds of arms, and actually saveing her from the fire through his noble chivalry. This connection involved him in a long and cruel war with King Arthur; after whose death he became a hermit. His adventures, which take up a considerable portion of *Mort d'Arthur,* are the subject of a very old French romance, in three folio volumes, beside a number of MSS.

Kyng Ban-Booght, and kyng Bos, *
Of ham ther was a greet los,   20
   Men sawe tho no wher her make ;
Syr Galafre,† and syr Launfale,
Wherof a noble tale
   Among us schall awake.

With Artour ther was a bacheler,
And hadde ybe well many a yer,
   Launfal for soth he hyght,
He gaf gyftys largelyche,
Gold, and sylver, and clodes ryche,
   To squyer and to knyght.   30
For hys largesse and hys bountè,
The kynges stuward made was he,
   Ten yer, y you plyght ;
Of alle the knyghtes of the table rounde
So large ther was noon yfounde,
   Be dayes ne be nyght,

So hyt be fyll, yn the tenthe yer,
Marlyn was Artours counsalere,‡
   He radde hym for to wende

---

* *Ban* was king of *Benoic*, and *Boort* (not *Boozt*) king of *Gannes*. They were brothers, and both knights of the rounnd table. *Ban* was the father of sir Lancelot. *Boort* in *Mort d'Arthur* is called *Bors*. There is no king *Bos*: nor, in fact, do any of these names occur in the French original. There was, indeed, another *Boort*, or *Bors*, afterwards king of *Benoic ;* but the translator has evidently missupposed *Ban-Boozt* to be the name of one king, and *Bos* that of the other. A *"roman des rois* Bans and Beors *freres germains."* fo. is among the MSS. of the French national library. (*Bib. du roi*, 7184).

† No such name occurs among the knights of the round table, or is to be met with in any old romance. It is, probably, a corruption of *Galehaut, Galahalt*, or *Galahad*, of whom mention is made in *Mort d'Arthur*.

‡ Merlin, a powerful magician, was begotten by a devil, or incubus, upon a young damsel of great beauty, and daughter, as Geoffrey of Monmouth asserts, to the king of Demetia. He removed, by a wonderful machine of his own invention, the giants-dance, now Stone-henge, from Ireland, to Salisbury-plain, where part of it is still standing ; and, in order to enable Uther Pendragon, king of Britain, to enjoy Igerna, the wife of Gorlois, Duke of Cornwall, transformed him, by magical art, into the likeness of her husband ; which amorous connection, (Igerna being rendered an honest woman by the murder of her spouse, and timely intermarriage with king Uther,) enlightened the world, like another Alcmena, with a second Hercules, *videlicet*, the illustrious Arthur. This famous prophet, being violently enamoured of a fairy damsel, in the march of Little-Britain, named *Airvienne*, or *Viviane*, alias *The Lady* or *Damsel of the lake*, taught her so many of his magic secrets, that,

To king Ryon of Irlond ryght,*   40
And sette him ther a lady bryght,
   Gwennere hys doughtyr hende.
So he dede, and home her brought,
But syr Launfal lyked her noght,
   Ne other knyghtes that wer hende ;
For the lady bar los of swych word,
That sche hadde lemannys unther her lord,
   So fele ther nas noon ende.

They wer ywedded, as y you say,
Upon a Wytsonday,   50
   Before princes of moch pryde,
No man ne may telle yn tale
What tolk ther was at that bredale,
   Of countreys fer and wyde.
No nother man was yn halle ysette,
But he wer prelat, other baronette, †
   In herte ys naght to hyde,

---

once upon a time, she left him asleep in a cave within the perilous forest of
Darnantes, on the borders of the sea of Cornwall, and the sea of *Soreloys,*
where, if the credible inhabitants of those countries may be believed, he still
remains in that condition ; the place of his repose being effectually sealed by
force of grand conjurations, and having himself been never seen by any man, who
could give intelligence of it ; even that courteous knight Sir Gawin, who, after his
enchantment, had some conversation with him, not being permitted the gratification
of a single look. (See *Lancelot du lac,* fo. 6.) Her enchantments, however, are
related with some difference, and more particularity, in the romance of her venerable
gallant, or, rather, unfortunate dupe, *tome* 2, fo. 127, whereby it appears that, after
being enchanted by his mistress, as aforesaid he found himself, when he awoke, in the
strongest tower in the world, to wit, in the forest of *Broceliande,* whence he was never
able to depart, although she continued to visit him both by day and night at her
pleasure. The divine Ariosto, by poetical licence, has placed the tomb of this
magician in some part of France ; and our admirable Spenser, after an old tradition,
in Wales, which, in fact, seems to have had the best title to him. His prophecies,
which were first published in *The British History,* have since gone through repeated
editions, in Latin, French, and English.

* This king *Ryon,* or *Ryence,* was also king of North Wales, and of many isles. He
sent to King Arthur, for his beard, to enable him, with those of eleven other kings,
whom he had already discomfited, to purfle his mantle. See *Mort d'Arthur,* B. 1.
C. 24. According, however, to Geoffrey of Moumouth, this insulting message
proceeded from the giant *Ritho,* whom Arthur slew upon the mountain *Aravius.*
Ryon was afterwards brought prisoner to Arthur (C. 34); and is named among the
knights of the round-table. The author is singular in making Guenever his daughter.

† There was no *baronet,* properly so called, before the reign of James the first.
The word, at the same time, is by no means singular in ancient historians; but
whether a diminutive of *baron,* or a corruption of *banneret,* is uncertain.

Yf they ſatte noght alle ylyche,*
Har ſervyſe was good and ryche,
    Certeyn yn ech a ſyde.   60

And whan the lordes hadde ete yn the halle,
And the clothes wer drawen alle,
    As ye mowe her and lythe,
The botelers fentyn wyn,
To alle the lords that wer theryn,
    With chere both glad and blythe.
The quene yaf gyftes for the nones,
Gold and ſelver, precyous ſtonys,
    Her curtaſye to kythe,
Everych knyght ſche yaf broche, other ryng,   70
But ſyr Launfal ſche yaf no thyng,
    That grevede hym many a ſythe.

And whan the bredale was at ende
Launfal tok his leve to wende
    At Artour the kyng,
And ſeyde a lettere was to hym come,
That deth hadde hys fadyr ynome,
    He most to his beryynge.
Tho ſeyde king Artour, that was hende,
Launfal, if thou wylt fro me wende,   80
    Tak with the greet ſpendyng,
And my ſuster ſones two,
Bothe they ſchull with the go,
    At hom the for to bryng.

Launfal tok leve, withoute fable,
With knyghtes of the rounde table,
    And wente forth yn his journè,
Tyl he come to Karlyoun,†
To the meyrys hous of the toune,
    Hys ſervaunt that hadde ybe.   90

---

* The original reading is "ylyke."

† Caerleon (the *Urbs Legionum* of Geoffrey), formerly in Glamorganshire, but now in Monmouthshire, upon the river Uſk, near the Severn-ſea. The district, in which this city ſtood, was called *Gwent*, of which Arthur is ſaid to have been king. See Carte. *Caerlegion*, or *Caer Lheon (Civitas Legionum)*, is, likewiſe, the ancient name of Chester upon Dee. There is nothing of this in the original.

The meyr stod, as ye may here,
And saw hym come ride up anblere,
  With two knyghtes and other maynè,
Agayns hym he hath wey ynome,
And seyde, Syr, thou art well come,
  How faryth our kyng? tel me.

Launfal answerede and seyde than,
He faryth as well as any man,
  And elles greet ruthe hyt wore ;
But, syr meyr, without lesyng,   100
I am thepartyth fram the kyng,
  And that rewyth me sore :
Ne ther thar noman benethe ne above,
For the kyng Artours love,
  Onowre me never more ;
But, syr meyr, y pray the pur amour,
May y take with the sojour ?
  Som tyme we knewe us yore.

The meyr stod, and bethogte hym there,
What myght be hys answere,   110
  And to hym than gan he sayn,
Syr, seven knyghtes han her har in ynome,
And ever y wayte whan they wyl come,
  They arn of Lytyll-Bretayne.*
Launfal turnede hymself and lowgh,
Therof he hadde scorn inowgh,
  And seyde to his knyghtes tweyne,
Now may ye se swych ys service,
Unther a lord of lytyll pryse,
  How he may therof be fayn.   120

---

* Little-Britain, or Britany, called, by the French, *Basse-Bretagne*, and, by the ancients, Armorica, on the coast of France, opposite to Great Britain, where certain refugee Britons are said to have fled, and established a settlement, on the success of the Saxons, in or about the year 513. See Vertot's *Critical history*, &c. I, 103. Bede, however, by some strange mistake, supposes the Southern Britons to have proceeded *from* Armorica. There was a succession of British kings in this little territory, who are famous in the old French annals. These British emigrants seem to have been chiefly Cornish, not only from their having given the name of *Cornwall* to a part of their new acquisition, where they, likewise, had, as in their old possessions, a *Mount St. Michael,* but from the affinity of the two dialects, one of which is extant in its literary remains, and the other is still spoken.

Launfal awayward gan to ryde,
The meyr bad he schuld abyde,
   And seyde yn thys manere,
Syr, yn a chamber by my orchard-syde,
Ther may ye dwell with joye and pryde,
   Yf hyt your wyll were.
Launfal anoon ryghtes,
He and hys two knytes,
   Sojournede ther yn fere,
So savagelych hys good he besette,   130
That he ward yn greet dette,
   Ryght yn the ferst yere.

So hyt befell at Pentecost,
Swych tyme as the holy gost
   Among mankend gan lyght,
That syr Hugh and syr Jon,
Tok her leve for to gon
   At syr Launfal the knyght.
They seyd, Syr, our robes beth to-rent
And your tresour* ys all yspent,   140
   And we goth ewyll ydyght.
Thanne seyde syr Launfal to the knyghtes fre,
Tell yd no man of my povertè,
   For the love of god almyght.

The knyghtes answerede and seyde tho,
That they nolde him wreye never mo,
   All thys world to wynne.
With that word they† wente hym fro.
To Glastyngbery bothe two,
   Ther kyng Artour was inne.   150
The kyng sawe the knyghtes hende,
And ayens ham he gan wende,
   For they wer of his kenne ; ‡
Noon other robes they ne hadde
Than they out with ham ladde,
   And tho wete to-tore and thynne.

* The original reads : " tofour."
† The original reads : " the."
‡ Kin (?)

Than seyde quene Gwenore, that was fel
How faryth the proud knight Launfal ?
   May he hys armes welde ?
Ye, madame, sayde the knytes than,   160
He faryth as well as any man,
   And ellys god hyt schelde.
Moche worchyp and greet honour,
To Gonore the quene and King Artour,
   Of syr Launfal they telde ;
And seyde, He lovede us so,
That he would us evermo,
   At wyll have yhelde.

But upon a rayny day hyt befel,
An huntynge wente syr Launfel,   170
   To chasy yn holtes hore,
In our old robes we yede that day,
And thus we beth ywent away,
   As we before hym wore.
Glad was Artour the kyng,
That Launfal was yn good lyking,
   The quene hyt rew well sore ;
For sche wold, with all her myght,
That he hadde be, bothe day and nyght,
   In paynys mor and more.   180

Upon a day of the trinitè,
A feste of greet solempnitè
   In Carlyoun was holde,
Erles and barones of that countrè.
Ladyes and borjaes * of that citè,
   Thyder come bothe yongh and old.
But Launfal for hys povertè
Was not bode to that semblè,
   Lyte men of hym tolde ;
The meyr to the feste was of sent,   190
The merys doughter to Launfal went,
   And axede yf he wolde

In halle dyne with her that day.
Damesele, he sayde, nay,
   To dyne have i no herte ;

* Fr. Bourgeois.

B

Thre dayes ther ben agon
Mete ne drynke eet y noon,
   And all was for povert.
To-day to cherche y wold have gon,
But me fawtede * hosyn and schon,   200
   Clenly brech and scherte ;
And for defawte of clodynge,
Ne myghte y yn with the peple thrynge,
   No wonther dough me smerte

But othyng, damesele, y pray the,
Sadel and brydel lene thou me,
   A whyle for to ryde,
That y myghte comfortede be.
By a launde unther thys cyte,
   Al yn thys undern-tyde.   210
Launfal dyghte hys courser,
Without knave other squyer,
   He rood with lytyll pryde ;
Hys hors slod, and fel yn the fen,
Wherfore hym scornede many men,
   Abowte hym fer and wyde.

Poverly the knyght to hors gan sprynge,
For to dryve away lokynge,
   He rood toward the west ;
The wether was hot the undern-tyde,
He lyghte adoun, and gan abyde,   220
   Under a fayr forest :
And for hete to the wedere,
Hys mantell he feld togydere,
   And sette hym doun to reste ;
Thus sat the knyght yn symplyte,
In the schadowe unther a tre,
   Ther that hym lykede best.

As he sat yn sorrow and sore,
He sawe come out of holtes hore   230
   Gentyll maydenes two,
Har kertoles wer of Inde sandel,
Ilased smalle, jolyf and well,
   Ther myght noon gayer go.

---

* Failed.

Har manteles wer of grene felwet,
Ybordured with gold, right well ysette
　　Ipelvred with grys and gro ;
Har heddys wer dyght well withalle,
Everych hadde oon a jolyf coronall,
　　Wyth syxty gemmys and mo.　　　　240

Har faces wer whyt as snow on downe,
Har rode was red, her eyn wor browne,
　　I sawe never non swyche ;
That oon bar of gold a basyn,
That other a towayle whyt and fyn,
　　Of selk that was good and ryche.
Her kercheves wer well schyre,
Arayd wyth ryche gold wyre,
　　Launfal began to syche ;
They com to hym over the hoth,　　　　250
He was curteys, aud ayens hem goth,
　　And greette hem myldelyche.

Damesels, he seyde, god yow se !
Syr knyght, they seyde, well the be !
　　Our lady, dame Tryamour,
Bad thou schuldest com speke with here,
Gyf hyt wer thy wylle, sere,
　　Wythoute more sojour.
Launfal hem grauntede curteyslyche,
And wente wyth hem myldelyche,　　　　260
　　They wheryn whyt as flour ;
And when they come in the forest an hygh,
A pavyloun yteld he sygh,
　　With merthe and mochell honour.

The pavyloun was wrouth for sothe, y wys,
All of werk of Sarsynys,
　　The pomelles of crystall ;
Upon the toppe an ern ther stod
Of bournede gold ryche and good,
　　Iflorysched with ryche amall.　　　　270
Hys eyn wer carbonkeles bryght,
As the mone they schon* a-nyght,
　　That spreteth out ovyr all ;

---

* The original reads : "theschon."

Alysaundre the conquerour,
Ne kyng Artour, yn hys most honour,
   Ne hadde noon scwych juell.

He fond yn the pavyloun
The kynges doughter of Olyroun,*
   Dame Tryamour,† that hyghte,
Her fadyr was kyng of fayrye, ‡   280
Of occient fer and nyghe,
   A man of mochell myghte.
In the pavyloun he fond a bed of prys,
Iheled with purpur bys,
   That semylé was of syghte,
Therinne lay that lady gent,
That after syr Launfal hedde ysent,
   That lefsome lemede bryght.

For hete her clothes down she dede,
Almest to her gerdyl stede,   290
   Than lay sche uncovert ;
Sche was as whyt as lylye yn May,
Or snow that sneweth yn wynterys day,
   He seygh never non so pert .
The rede rose, whan she ys newe,
Ayens her rode nes naught of hewe,
   I dar well say yn sert¹;
Her here schon as gold wyre,
May no man rede here atyre,
   Ne naught well thenke yn hert.   300

---

* Oleron is an isle of France, on the coast of Aunis, and of Saintonge. It was known to the ancients under the name of *Uliarus*, as appears from Pliny. Sidonius Appollinaris calls it *Olario*. The maratime laws of France and England hence received the appellation they still retain of *La ley Olyron* ; and here it was that King Richard the first stopped, in his return from the Holy Land, to correct them. In 1047 it belonged to Geoffrey de Martel, earl of Anjou, and Agnes his wife. See Martiniere, and Cokes, 4*th institute*, 144.

   † This lady's name is not mentioned in the original. *Tryamour*, at the same time, is, elsewhere, that of a knight, and the subject of a metrical romance, certainly from the French.

   ‡ The following description of a female fay, or fairy, is given in the romance of *Lancelot du lac*, Paris, 1533, fo. C. 8.

   " *La damoiselle qui Lancelot porta au lac estoit une* fée, *et en celluy temps estoient appellees* faées *toutes celles qui sentremettoient d'enchantements et de charmes. . . et scavoient la force et la vertu des parolles, des pierres, et des herbes, parquoy elles estoient tenue en jeunesse et en*

Sche seyde, Launfal my lemman swete,
Al my joye for the y lete,
   Swetyng paramour,
Ther nys no man yn Cristentè,
That y love so moche as the,
   Kyng, neyther emperour.
Launfal beheld that swete wyghth,
All hys love yn her was lyghth,
   And keste that swete flour ;
And sat adoun her besyde,
And seyde, Swetyng, what so betydc,
   I am to thyn honour.

She seyde, Syr knyght, gentyl and hende,
I wot thy stat, ord, and ende,
   Be naught aschamed of me ;
Yf thou wylt truly to me take,
And alle wemen for me forsake,
   Ryche i wyll make the.
I wyll the yeve an alner,
Imad of sylk and of gold cler,   320
   Wyth fayre ymages thre ;
As oft thou puttest the hond therinne,
A mark of gold thou schalt wynne,
   In wat place that thou be.

Also, sche seyde, syr Launfal,
I yeve the Blaunchard my stede lel,

---

beaulté, et en grandes richesses comment elles devisoient." These fairies, not unfrequent in the old romances, united the ideas of power and beauty ; and it is to such a character that Shakspeare alludes, where he makes Anthony to say of CLEOPATRA,
    "To this GREAT FAIRY I'll commend thy acts."
Milton, too, appears to have had an accurate notion upon this subject :
    " Nymphs of Diana's train, and Naiades,
      And ladies of th' Hesperides, that seem'd,
      Fairer than feign'd of old, or fabl'd since
      Of fairy damsels met in forest wide
      By knights of Logres, or of Lyones,
      Lancelot, or Pelleas, or Pellenore."
It is perfect ignorance to confound the fairies of romance either with the pigmy race of that denomination, of whom the same great poet has given a beautiful and correct description, or with the fanciful creation of Spencer.

And Gyfre my owen knave ; *
And of my armes oo pensel,
Wyth thre ermyns ypented well, 330
   Also thou schalt have.
In werre, ne yn turnement,
Ne schall the greve no knyghtes dent,
   So well y schall the save.
Than answerede the gentyl knyght,
And seyde, Gramarcy, my swete wyght,
   No bettere kepte y have.

The damesell gan her up sette,
And bad her maydenes her fette,
   To hyr hondys watyr clere ; 340
Hyt was ydo without lette,
The cloth was spred, the bord was sette,
   They wente to have sopere.
Mete and drynk they hadde afyn,
Pyement, clare and Reynysch wyn,
   And elles greet wondyr hyt wer ;
Whan they had sowpeth, and the day was gon,
They wente to bedde, and that anoon,
   Launfal and sche yn fere.

For play lytyll they sclepte that nyght, 350
Tyll on morn hyt was day-lyght,
   She badd hym aryse anoon ;
Hy seyde to hym, Syr gentyl knyght,
And thou wilt speke with me any wyght,
   To a derne stede thou gon.
Well privyly i woll come to the,
No man alyve ne schall me se,
   As stylle as any ston.
Tho was Launfal glad and blythe,
He cowde no man hys joye kythe, 360
   And keste her well good won.

---

* No such names occur in the original. Giflet (or Girflet) *le fltz* Mu (*alias* Do) is
a character in the o'd French romance of *Lancelot du lac.*

But of othyng, syr knyght, i warne the,
That thou make no bost of me,
    For no kennes mede ;
And yf thou doost, y warny the before,
All my love thou hast forlore :
    And thus to hym sche seyde.
Launfal tok hys leve to wende,
Gyfre kedde that he was hende,
    And brought Launfal hys stede ;   370
Launfal lepte ynto the arsoun,
And rood hom to Karlyoun,
    In hys pover wede.

Tho was the knyght yn herte at wylle,
In his chaunber he hyld him stylle,
    All that undern-tyde ;
Than come ther thorwgh the cyté ten
Well yharneysyth men
    Upon ten somers ryde.
Some wyth sylver, some wyth gold,   380
All to syr Launfal hyt schold,
    To presente hym wyth pryde ;
Wyth ryche clothes and armure bryght,
They axede aftyr Launfal the knyght,
    Whar he gan abyde.

The yong men wer clodeth yn Ynde,
Gyfre he rood all behynde,
    Up Blaunchard whyt as flour ;
Tho seyde a boy, that yn the market stod,
How fer schall all thys good ?   390
    Tell us pur amour.
Tho seyde Gyfre, Hyt ys ysent
To syr Launfal yn present,
    That hath leved yn greet dolour.
Than seyde the boy, Nys he but a wrecche ?
What thar any man of hym recche ?*
    At the meyrys hous he taketh sojour.

---

* Mr. Ellis, who published this romance, for the first time at the end of the
second volume of "the *fabliaux* or tales" of his deceased friend, G. L. Way,
Esq., has strangely misconceived this simple passage ; supposing AWRECHE, as it is

At the merys hous they gon alyghte,
And presented the noble knyghte
   Wyth swych good as hym was sent ;
And whan the meyr seygh that rychesse,
And syr Launfales noblenesse,
   He held hym self foule yschent.
Tho seyde the meyr, Syr, pur charyte,
In halle to day that thou wylt ete with me,
   Yesterday y hadde yment
At the feste we wolde han be yn same,
And y hadde solas and game,
   And erst thou were ywent.

"Syr meyr, god foryelde the,   410
Whyles y was yn my poverté,
   Thou bede me never dyne :
Now y have more gold and fe,
That myne frendes han sent me,
   Than thou and alle dyne."
The meyr for schame away yede,
Launfal yn purpure gan hym schrede,
   Ipelvred with whyt ermyne ;
All that Launfal had borwyth before
Gyfre, be tayle and be score,   420
   Yald hyt well and fyne.

Launfal helde ryche festes,
Fyfty fedde povere gestes,
   That in myscaef wer ;
Fyfty boughte stronge stedes,
   Fyfty yaf ryche wedes,
      To knyghtes and squyere,
Fyfty rewardede relygyons.
Fyfty delyverede povere prysouns,
   And made ham quyt and schere :   430
Fyfty clodede gestours,
To many men he dede honours,
   In countreys fer and nere.

---

there printed to be one word, and the meaning, " He is not without his REVENGE (*i.e.,*
COMPENSATION) whatever any man may think of him." The boy, however, mani-
festly intends our seedy knight no compliment in the question he asks—" Is he
aught," says he, " but a wretch (or beggarly rascal ?) What does anyone care for
him ? "

Alle the lordes of Karlyoun
Lette crye a turnement yn the toun,
   For love of syr Launfel,
And for Blaunchard, hys good stede,
To wyte how hym wold spede,
   That was ymade so well.
And whan the day was ycome,   440
That the justes were yn ynome,
   They ryde out al so snell,
Trompours gon har bemes blowe,
The lordes ryden out a-rowe.
   That were yn castell.

Ther began the turnement,
And ech knyght leyd on other good dent,
   Wyth mases and wyth swerdes bothe ;
Me myghte ysé some, therfore
Stedes ywonne, and some ylore,   450
   And knyghtes* wonther wroghth.
Syth the rounde table was
A bettere turnement ther nas,
   I dar well say for sothe,
Many a lorde of Karlyoun
That day were ybore adoun,
   Certayn withouten othe.

Of Karlyoun the ryche constable
Rod to Launfall, without fable,
   He nolde no lengere abyde ;   460
He smot to Launfal, and he to hym,
Well sterne strokes, and well grym,
   Ther wer in eche a syde.
Launfal was of hym yware,
Out of his sadell he hym bar,
   To grounde that ylke tyde,
And whan the constable was bore adoun,
Gyfre lepte ynto the arsoun,
   And awey he gan to ryde.

---

* The original reading is " kyztes."

The erl of Chestere thereof segh,   470
For wrethe yn herte he was wod negh,
   And rood to syr Launfale,
And smot hym yn the helm on hegh.
That the crest adoun flegh,
   Thus seyd the Frenssch tale.
Launfal was mochel of myght,
Of hys stede he did hym lyght,
   And bar hym doun yn the dale ;
Than come ther syr Launfal abowte
Of Walssche knyghtes a greet rowte,   480
   The numbre y not how fale.

Than myghte me se scheldes ryve,
Speres to-breste and to-dryve,
   Behynde and ek before,
Thorugh Launfal and hys stedes dent,
Many a knyght, verement,
   To ground was ibore.
So the prys of that turnay
Was delyvered to Launfal that day,
   Without oth yswore ;   490
Launfal rod to Karlyoun.
To the meyrys hous yn the toun,
   And many a lord hym before.

And than the noble knyght Launfal
Helde a feste ryche and ryall,
   That leste fourtenyght,
Erles and barouns fale
Semely wer sette yn sale,
   And ryaly were adyght.
And every day dame Triamour,   500
Sche com to syr Launfal bour,
   A day when hyt was nyght,
Of all that ever wer ther tho,
Segh he non bot they two,
   Gyfre and Launfal the knyght.

LAUNFAL.

PART II.

A knyght ther was yn Lumbardye,*
To syr Launfal hadde he greet envye,
   Syr Valentyne he hyghte ;
He herde speke of syr Launfal,
That he couth justy well,   510
   And was a man of mochel myghte.
Syr Valentyne was wonther strong,
Fyftene feet he was longe,
   Hym thoghte he brente bryghte
Bnt he myghte with Launfal pleye,
In the feld betwene ham tweye,
   To justy, other to fyghte.

Syr Valentyne sat yn hys halle,
Hys massengere he let ycalle,
   And seyde he moste wende   520
To syr Launfal the noble knyght,
That was yholde so mychel of myght,
   To Bretayne he wolde hym sende ;
And sey hym, for love of hys lemman,
Yf sche be any gentyle woman,
   Courteys, fre, other hende,
That he come with me to juste,
To kepe hys harneys from the ruste,
   And elles hys manhood schende.

---

* This episode, the introduction of the mayor of Carleon, and his daughter, even
the name of that place, and several other incidents, are entirely owing to the English
poet, there being nothing of this sort in the original.

The messengere ys forth ywent,   530
To tho hys lordys commaundement,
   He hadde wynde at wylle
Whan he was over the water ycome,
The way to Launfal he hath ynome,
   And grette hym with wordes stylle :
And seyd, Syr, my lord, syr Valentyne,
A noble werrour, and queynte of gynne,
   Hath me sent the tylle ;
And prayeth the, for thy lemmanes sake,
Thou schuldest with hym justes take.   540
   Tho lough Launfal full stylle.

And seyde, as he was gentyl knyght,
Thylke day a fourtenyght,
   He wold wyth hym play.
He yaf the messenger, for that tydyng,
A noble courser and a ryng,
   and a robe of ray,
Launfal tok leve at Tryamour,
That was the bryght berde yn bour,
   And keste that swete may ;   550
Thanne seyde that swete wyght,
Dreed the nothyng, syr gentyl knyght,
   Thou schalt hym sle that day.

Launfal nolde nothyng wyth hym have,
But Blaunchard hys stede, and Gyfre hys knave,
   Of all hys tayr maynè ;
He schyppede and hadde wynd well good,
And wente over the solte flod,
   Into Lumbardye.
Whan he was over the water ycome,   560
Ther the justes schulde be nome,
   In the cyté of Atalye,
Syr Valentyn hadde a greet ost,
And syr Launfal abatede her bost,
   Wyth lytyll cumpanye.

And whan syr Launfal was ydyght,
Upon Blaunchard hys stede lyght,
   With helm, and spere, and schelde,

All that sawe hym yn armes bryght,
And seyde they sawe never swych a knyght,   570
  That hym with eyen beheld.
Tho ryde togydere thes knyghtes two,
That har schaftes to-broste bo,
  And to-scyverede yn the felde ;
Another cours togedere they rod,
That syr Launfal helm of glod,
  In tale as hyt ys telde.

Syr Valentyn logh, and hadde good game,
Hadde Launfal never so moche schame,
  Beforhond yn no fyght ;   580
Gyfre kedde he was good at nede,
And lepte upon hys maystrys stede,
  No man ne segh with syght.
And er than thay togedere mette,
Hys lordes helm he on sette,
  Fayre and well adyght ;
Tho was Launfal glad and blythe,
And donkede Gyfre many syde,
  For hys dede so mochel of myght.

Syr Valentyne smot Launfal soo,   590
That hys scheld fel hym fro,
  Anoon ryght yn that stounde ;
And Gyfre the scheld up hente,
And broghte hyt hys lord to presente,
  Er hyt cam thoune to grounde.
Tho was Launfal glad and blythe,
And rode ayen the thrydde syde,
  As a knyght of mochel mounde ;
Syr Valentyne he smot so there,
That hors and mon bothe deed were,   600
  Gronyng wyth grysly wounde.

Alle the lordes of Atalye
To syr Launfal hadde greet envye,
  That Valentyne was yslawe,

And swore that he schold dye,
Er he wente out of Lumbardye,
   And be hongede, and to-drawe.
Syr Launfal brayde out hys fachon,
And as lyght as dew he leyde hem dounc,
   In a lytyll drawe,   610
And whan he hadde the lordes selayn,
He went ayen ynto Bretayn,
   Wyth solas and wyth plawc.

The tydyng com to Artour the kyng,
Anoon wythout lesyng,
   Of syr Launfales noblcssc,
Anoon a letter to hym sende,
That Launfal schuld to hym wende,
   At seynt Jonnys masse.
For kyng Artour would a feste holde,   620
Of erles and of barouns bolde,
   Of lordynges more and lesse ;
Syr Launfal schud be stward of hallc,
For to agye hys gestes alle,
   For cowthe of largesse.

Launfal toke leve at Tryamour,
For to wende to kyng Artour,
   Hys feste for to agye,
Ther he fond merthe and moch honour,
Ladyes that wer well bryght yn bour,   630
   Of knyghtes greet cumpanye.
Fourty dayes leste the feste,
Ryche, ryall, and honeste,
   What help hyt for to lye ?
And at the fourty dayes ende,
The lordes toke har leve to wende,
   Everych yn hys partye.

And aftyr mete syr Gaweyn,
Syr Gyeryes, and Agrafayn,
   And syr Launfal also,   640

Wente to daunce upon the grene,
Unther the tour ther lay the quene,
　　Wyth syxty ladyes and mo.
To lede the daunce Launfale was set,
For hys largesse he was lovede the bet,
　　Sertayn of alle tho ;
The quene lay out and beheld hem alle,
I se, sche seyde, daunce large Launfalle,
　　To hym than wyll y go.

Of alle the knyghtes that ye se there,　　　650
He ys the fayreste bachelere,
　　He ne hadde never no wyf ;
Tyde me good, other ylle,
I wyll go and wyte hys wylle,
　　Y love hym as my lyf.
Sche tok with her a companye,
The fayrest that sche myghte aspye,
　　Syxty ladyes and fyf,
And went hem doun anoon ryghtes,
Ham to pley among the knyghtes,　　　660
　　Well stylle wythouten stryf.

The quene yede to the formeste ende,
Betwene Launfal and Gauweyn the hende,
　　And after her ladyes bryght,
To daunce they wente alle yn same,
To se hem play hyt was fayr game,
　　A lady and a knyght.
They hadde menstrales of moch honours,
Fydelers, sytolyrs, and trompours,
　　And elles hyt were unryght ;　　　670
Ther they playde, for sothe to say,
After mete the somerys day,
　　All what hyt was neygh nyght.

And whanne the daunce began to slake,
The quene gan Launfal to counsell take,
　　And seyde yn thys manere :
Sertaynlyche, syr knyght,
I have the lovyd wyth all my myght,
　　More than thys seven yere.

But that thou lovye me,   680
Sertes y dye for love of the,
   Launfal, my lemman dere.
Than answerede the gentyll knyght,
I nell be traytour thay ne nyght,
   Be god, that all may stere.

Sche seyde, Fy on the, thou coward,
An hongeth worth thou hye and hard,
   That thou ever were ybore,
That thou lyvest hyt ys pytè,
Thou lovyst no woman, ne no woman the,   690
   Thow wer worthy forlore.
The knyght was sore aschamed tho,
To speke ne myghte he forgo,
   And seyde the quene before :
I have loved a fayryr woman,
Than thou ever leydest thy ney upon,
   Thys seven yer and more.

Hyr lothlokste mayde, wythoute wene,
Myghte bet be a quene
   Than thou in all thy lyve.   700
Therfore the quene was swythe wroght,
Sche taketh hyr maydenes, and forth hy goth,
   Into her tour also blyve,
And anon sche ley doun yn hyr bedde,
For wrethe syk sche hyr bredde,
   And swore, so moste sche thryve,
Sche wold of Launfal be so awreke,
That all the lond schuld of hym speke,
   Wythinne the dayes fyfe.

King Artour com fro huntynge,   710
Blythe and glad yn all thyng,
   To hys chamber than wente he,
Anoone the quene on hym gan crye,
But y be awreke, y schall dye,
   Myn herte wyll breke athre,

I spak to Launfal yn my game,
And he besofte me of schame,
   My lemman for to be ;
And of a lemman hys yelp he madc,
That the lodlokest mayde that sche haddc   720
   Myght be a quene above me.

Kyng Artour was well worth,
And be god he swor hys oth,
   That Launfal schuld be slawe ;
He wente aftyr doghty knyghtes,
To brynge Launfal anoon ryghtes,
   To be hongeth and to-drawe.
The knyghtes softe hym anoon,
But Launfal was to hys chamber gon,
   To han hadde solas and plawe ;   730
He softe hys leef, but sche was lore,
As sche hadde warnede hym before,
   Tho was Launfal unfawe.

He lokede yn hys alner,
That fond hym spendyng all plener,
   Whan that he hadde nede,
And ther nas noon, for soth to say,
And Gyfre was yryde away,
   Up[on] Blaunchard hys stede.
All that he hadde before ywonne,   740
Hyt malt as snow ayens the sunne,
   In romaunce as we rede ;
Hys armur, that was whyt as flour,
Hyt becom of blak colour,
   And thus than Launfal seyde :

Alas, he seyde, my creature,
How schall i from the endure,
   Swetyng Tryamour ?
All my joye i have forlore,
And the that me ys worst sore,   750
   Thou blysful berde yn bour.*

---

* "These two lines," at least in Mr. Ellis's edition, he says, "are rather obscure ;"
but that obscurity was merely occasioned by his printing THAN for THOU. The
perspicacious editor, nevertheless, saw how the original must have been. Another
typographical error, in that edition, has been the cause of his explaining *soth* (mis-
printed *for*) by *sure*.

He bet hys body and hys hedde ek,
And cursede the mouth that he wyth spek,
   Wyth care and greet dolour ;
And, for sorow, yn that stounde,
Anoon he fell aswowe to grounde ;
   Wyth that come knyghtes four,

And bond hym, and ladde hym tho,
Tho was the knyghte yn doble wo,
   Before Artour the kyng.   760
Than seyde kyng Artour,
Fyle ataynte traytour !
   Why madest thou swyche yelpyng?
That thy lemmannes lodlokest mayde
Was fayrer than my wyf, thou seyde,
   That was a fowl lesynge ;
And thou besoftest her before than,
That sche schold be thy lemman,
   That was mysprowd lykynge.

The knyght answerede, with egre mode,   770
Before the kyng ther he stode,
   The quene on hym gan lye :
" Sethe that y ever was yborn.
I besofte her here beforn
   Never of no folye.
But sche seyde y nas no man,
Ne that me lovede no woman,
   Ne no womannes companye ;
And i answerede her and sayde,
That my lemmannes lodlekest mayde   780
   To be a quene was better wordye.

Sertes, lordynges, hyt ys so,
I am a redy for to tho
   All that the court wyll loke.
To say the soth, wythout les,
All togedere how hyt was,
   Twelve knyghtes wer dryve to boke.
All they seyde ham betwene,
That knewe the maners of the quene,
   And the queste toke ;   790

The quene bar los of swych a word,
That sche lovede lemmannes wythout her lord,
　　Har never on hyt forsoke.

Therfor they seyden alle,
Hyt was long on the quene, and not on Launfal,
　　Therof they gonne hym skere ;
And yf he myghte hys lemman brynge,
That he made of swych yelpynge,
　　Other the maydenes were
Bryghtere than the quene of hewe,　　　　　800
Launfal schuld be holde trewe,
　　Of that yn all manere ;
And yf he myghte not brynge hys lef,
He schud be hongede as a thef,
　　They seyden all yn fere.

Alle yn fere they made proferynge,
That Launfal schuld hys lemman brynge :
　　Hys heed he gan to laye.
Than seyde the quene, wythout lesynge,
Yyf he bryngeth a fayrer thynge,　　　　　810
　　Put out my eeyn gray.
Whan that wajowr was take on honde,
Launfal therto two borwes fonde,
　　Noble knyghtes twayn,
Syr Percevall, and syr Gawayn,
They wer hys borwes, soth to sayn,
　　Tyll a certayn day.

The certayn day, i yow plyght,
Was twelve moneth and fourtenyght,
　　That he schuld hys lemman brynge ;　　820
Syr Launfal, that noble knyght,
Greet sorow and care yn hym was lyght,
　　Hys hondys he gan wrynge.
So greet sorowe hym was upan,
Gladlyche hys lyf he wold a forgon,
　　In care and in marnynge ;
Gladlyche he wold hys hed forgo,
Everych man therfore was wo,
　　That wyste of that tydynge.

The certayn day was nyghyng,　　　　830
Hys borowes hym broght befor the kyng,
　　The kyng recordede tho,
And bad hym bryng hys lef yn syght,
Syr Launfal seyde that he ne myght,
　　Therfore hym was well wo.
The kyng commaundede the barouns alle,
To yeve jugement on Launfal,
　　And dampny hym to sclo.
Than sayde the erl of Cornewayle,
That was wyth ham at that counceyle,　　840
　　We wyllyd naght do so :

Greet schame hyt wor us alle upon
For to dampny that gentylman,
　　That hath be hende and fre ;
Therfor, lordynges, doth be my reed,
Our kyng, we wyllyth another wey lede,
　　Out of lond|Launfal schall fle.
And as they stod thus spekynge,
The barouns sawe come rydynge
　　Ten maydenes bryght of ble,　　　　850
Ham thoghte they were so bryght and schene,
That the lodlokest, wythout wene,
　　Har quene than myghte be.

Tho seyde Gawayn, that corteys knyght,
Launfal, brodyr, drede the no wyght,
　　Her cometh thy lemman hende.
Launfal answerede, and seyde Y wys,
Non of ham my lemman nys,
　　Gawayn, my lefly frende.
To that castell they wente ryghte,　　860
At the gate they gonne alyght,
　　Befor kyng Artour gonne they wende,
And bede hym make a redy hastyly
A fayr chamber for her lady,
　　That was come of kinges kende.

Ho ys your lady ?　Artour seyde.
Ye schull y wyte, seyde the mayde,
　　For sche cometh ryde.

The kyng commaundede, for her sake,
The fayryst chaunber for to take,   870
   In hys palys that tyde.
And anon to hys barouns he sente,
For to yeve jugemente
   Upon that traytour full of pryde ;
The barouns answerede, anoon ryght,
Have we seyn the madenes bryght,
   Whe schull not longe abyde.

A newe tale they gonne tho,
Some of wele, and some of wo,
   Har lord the kyng to queme,   880
Some dampnede Launfal there,
And some made hym quyt and skere,
   Har tales wer well breme.
Tho saw they other ten maydenes bryght,
Fayryr than the other ten of syght,
   As they gone hym deme,
They ryd upon joly moyles of Spayne,
With sadell and brydell of Champayne,
   Her lorayns lyght gonne leme.

They wer yclodeth yn samyt tyre,   890
Ech man hadde greet desyre
   To se har clodynge.
Tho seyde Gaweyn, that curtayse knyght,
Launfal, her cometh thy swete wyght,
   That may thy bote brynge.
Launfal answerede, with drery doght,
And seyde, Alas, y knowe her noght,
   Ne non of all the ofsprynge.
Forth they wente to that palys,
And lyghte at the hye deys,   900
   Before Artour the kynge.

And grette the kyng and quene ek,
And oo mayde thys wordes spak,
   To the kyng Artour,
Thyn halle agrayde and hele the walles,
Wyth clodes and wyth ryche palles,
   Ayens my lady Tryamour.

The kyng answerede bedene,
Well come, ye maydenes schene,
    Be our lord the savyour.   910
He commaundede Launcelot du Lake to brynge hem
        yn fere,
In the chamber ther har felawes were,
    Wyth merthe and moche honour.

Anoon the quene suppose gyle
That Launfal schulld yn a whyle
    Be ymade quyt and skere,
Thorugh hys lemman that was commynge,
Anon sche seyde to Artour the kyng,
    Syre, curtays yf [thou] were,
Or yf thou lovedest thyn honour,   920
I schuld be awreke of that traytour,
    That doth me changy chere,
To Launfal thou schuldest not spare,
Thy barouns dryveth the to bysmare.
    He ys hem lef and dere.

And as the quene spak to the kyng,
The barouns seygh come rydynge
    A damesele alone,
Upoon a whyt comely palfrey,
They saw never non so gay,   930
    Upon the grounde gone.
Gentyll, jolyf, as bryd on bowe,
In all manere fayr inowe,
    To wonye yn worldly wone,
The lady was bryght as blosme on brere,
Wyth eyen gray, wyth lovelych chere,
    Her leyre lyght schoone.

As rose on rys her rode was red,
The her schon upon her hed,
    As gold wyre that schynyth bryght;   940
Sche hadde a croune upon her molde,
Of ryche stones and of golde,

That lossom lemede lyght.
The lady was clad yn purpere palle,
Wyth gentyll body and myddyl small,
 That semely was of syght ;
Her mantyll was furryth with whyt ermyn,
Ireversyd jolyf and fyn,
 No rychere be ne myght.

Her sadell was semyly sett,   950
The sambus wer grene felvet,
 Ipaynted with ymagerye,
The bordure was of belles,
Of ryche gold and nothing elles,
 That any man myghte aspye.
In the arsouns, before and behynde,
Were twey ftones of Ynde,
 Gay for the maystrye ;
The paytrelle of her palfraye,
Was worth an erldome, stoute and gay,   960
 The best yn Lumbardye.

A gerfawcon sche bar on her hond,
A softe pas her palfray fond,
 That men her schuld beholde ;
Thorugh Karlyon rood that lady,
Twey whyte grehoundys ronne hyr by,
 Har colers were of golde.
And whan Launfal sawe that lady,
To alle the folk he gon crye an hy,
 Both to yonge and olde,   970
Her, he seyde, comyth my lemman swete,
Sche myghte me of my balys bete,
 Yef that lady wolde.

Forth sche wente ynto the halle,
Ther was the quene and the ladyes alle,
 And also kyng Artour,
Her maydenes come ayens her ryght,
To take her styrop whan sche lyght,
 Of the lady dame Tyramour.

Sche dede of her mantyll on the flet,   980
That men schuld her beholde the bet,
     Wythoute a more sojour,
Kyng Artour gan her sayre grete,
And sche hym agayn, with wordes swete,
     That were of greet valour.

Up stod the quene and ladyes stoute,
Her for to beholde all aboute,
     How evene sche stod upryght ;
Than wer they wyth her also donne,
As ys the mone ayen the sonne,   990
     A day whan hyt ys lyght.
Than seyde sche to Artour the kyng,
Syr, hydyr i com for swych a thyng,
     To skere Launfal the knyght,
That he never, yn no folye,
Besofte the quene of no druryc,
     By dayes ne be nyght.

Therfor, syr kyng, good kepe thou myne,
He bad naght her, but sche bad hym,
     Here lemman for to be ;   1000
And he answerede her and seyde,
That hys lemmannes lothlokest mayde
     Was fayryr than was sche.
Kyng Artour seyde, wythoute nothe,
Ech may ysè that ys sothe,
     Bryghtere that ye be.
Wyth that dame Tryamour to the quene geth,
And blew on her swych a breth,
     That never eft myght sche se.

The lady lep an hyr palfray,   1010
And bad hem alle have good day,
     Sche nolde no lengere abyde ;
Wyth that com Gyfre all so prest,
Wyth Launfalys stede out of the forest,
     And stod Launfal besyde.
The knyght to horse began to sprynge,
Anoon wythout any lettynge,
     Wyth hys lemman away to ryde ;

The lady tok her maydenys achon,
And wente the way that sche hadde er gon,   1020
  Wyth solas and wyth pryde.

The lady rod dorth Cardevyle,
Fer ynto a jolyf ile,
  Olyroun that hyghte ;
Every yer upon a certayn day,
Me may here Launfales stede nay,
  And hym se with syght.
Ho that wyll there axsy justus,
To kepe hys armes fro the rustus,
  In turnement other fyght ;   1030
Dar he never forther gon,
Ther he may fynde justes anoon,
  Wyth syr Launfal the knyght.

Thus Launfal, wythouten fable,
That noble knyght of the rounde table,
  Was take yn to the fayrye ;
Seththe saw hym yn thys lond no man,
Ne no more of hym telle y ne can,
  For sothe, wythout lye.
Thomas Chestre made thys tale,   1040
Of the noble knyght syr Launfale,
  Good of chyvalrye.
Jhesus, that ys hevene kyng,
Yeve us alle hys blessyng,
  And hys modyr Marye !

LYBEAUS DISCONUS.*

THIS ancient romance is preserved in the Cotton MS. already mentioned, marked Caligula A. II. from which it is here given. About the latter half of another copy is in one of Sir Matthew Hales' MSS. in the library of Lincoln's Inn, apparently a different translation, but only containing, as usual, numberless various readings of little consequence; a third is said by Dr. Percy to be in his folio MS. It was certainly printed before the year 1600, being mentioned, by the name of "Libbius," in "Vertue's common wealth; or The highway to honour," by Henry Crosse, published in that year; and is even alluded to by Skelton, who died in 1529 :—

> "And of Sir Libius named Disconius."

The French original is unknown.

A story similar to that which forms the principal subject of the present poem may be found in the "Voiage and travaile of sir John Maundeville" (London, 1725, 8vo, p. 28). It, likewise, by some means, has made its way into a pretendedly ancient Northumberland ballad, entitled "The laidly worm of Spindleston-heugh," written, in reality, by Robert Lambe, vicar of Norham, author of "The history of chess," &c, who had, however, heard some old stanzas, of which he availed himself, sung by a maid-servant. The remote original of all these stories was, probably,

---

* i.e. *Le Beau desconnu,* or the fair unknown. The running-title is ever after uniformly *Desconus;* but the editor thought himself at liberty to follow the head, which bears *Disconus;* and had proceeded too far before he began to doubt the propriety of his conduct. It is never *Disconus* in the text. Mr. Tyrwhitt, however, so prints it.

much older than the time of Herodotus, by whom it is related (Urania).

Chaucer, in his "Rime of sire Thopas," among the "romances of pris" there enumerated, mentions those

"Of sire Libeaux and Pleindamour,"

(as Tyrwhitt reads after all the MSS. truly, and the old printed copies having Blandamoure, or Blaindamoure) ; upon which the learned and ingenious editor of the "Reliques of ancient English poetry," in the first three editions of that work, remarks that "As sir [Pleindamoure or] Blandamoure, no romance with this title has been discovered; but as the word occurs in that of *Libeaux*, 'tis possible Chaucer's memory deceived him : a remark, in which he is implicitly followed by his friend Warton, who says, "Of sir Blandamoure, I find nothing more than the name occurring in Sir Lebeaux" (History of English Poetry, I, 208) ; which he, most certainly, did not there find. "Even the titles of our old romances," he says, "such as Sir Blandamoure, betray their French extraction." (*Ib.* 139.) From the fourth and last edition, however, of the said Reliques, we now learn that the word in question is neither Pleindamoure nor Blandamoure, but Blaunde-mere, which is foreign to the purpose ; neither does any such name occur in the present copy ; nor, as the passage is carefully suppressed by the right reverend possessor, can one venture to imagine whether it be that of a man, a woman, or a horse.* This force of tergiversation has, to use the worthy prelate's own words, "destroyed all confidence."

Generally speaking, the Cotton MS. has *z* for *y* or *gh*, and *y* for *th*. The rhymes also of the third and sixth lines of every two stanzas are the same, except in a few instances, which have rendered it necessary to disregard that circumstance.

---

* This *venerabilisfimus episcopus* had the address to persuade a gentleman to whom he shewed his folio MS. and whose testimony was to convince the scepticism of the present editor, that he actually saw the word *Blandamoure*, which, it now turns out, does not exist ; though he would not suffer him to transcribe the line in which it occurred : he will easily recollect his name: upon a different occasion he gave Mr. Steevens a transcript from the above MS. of the vulgar ballad of *Old Simon the king*, with a strict injunction not to show it to this editor (who suspected, as the fact turned out, that he had sophisticated it, in a note to the last edition of Shakespeare), which, however, he immediately brought to him.

LYBEAUS DISCONUS.

JHESU CRYST, our savyour,
And hys modyr, that swete flowr,
  Helpe hem at her nede
That harkeneth of a conquerour,
Wys of wytte and whyght werrour,
  And doughty man in dede.
Hys name was called Geynleyn,
Beyete he was of syr Gaweyn,
  Be a forest syde ;
Of stouter knyght, and profytable,   10
Wyth Artour of the rounde table,*
  Ne herde ye never rede.

---

* This famous table, to which were attached one hundred knights, was the
property of Leodegrance, king of Camelard, who appears to have had it from
Uther Pendragon, for whom it had been made by the sorcerer Merlin, in token, as
the book says, of the roundness of the world, (or, according to his own romance), in
imitation of one established by Joseph of Arimathea, in the name of that which
Jesus had made at the supper of the twelve apostles, (see vol. I. fo. 40, &c.), and
came to king Arthur, as the portion of his wife Guenever, daughter of that monarch
Every knight had his seat, in which was his name, written in letters of gold.   One
of these was "the siege perillous," where no man was to sit but one: an honour
reserved for Sir Galaad, the son of Lancelot du Lake.   "King Arthur," according
to the history, "stablished all his knights, and gave them lands that were not rich
of land, and charged them never to do outrage nor murder, and always to fle treason.
Also, by no means, to be cruel, but to give mercy unto him that asked mercy, upon
paine of forfeiture of their worship, and lordship of king Arthur, for evermore, and
alway to do ladies, damosels, and gentlewomen, succour upon paine of death.   Also
that no man take no battailes in a wrong quarell for no law, nor for wordly goods.
Unto this were all the knights sworne of the round table, both old and young.'
Mort d'Arthur, Part I., C. 59.   It is not once mentioned by Geoffrey of Monmouth,

Thys Gynleyn was fayr of syght,
Gentyll of body, of face bryght,
    All bastard yef he were ;
Hys modyr kepte hym yn clos,
For douute of wykkede loos,
    As doughty chyld and dere.

And for love of hys fayr vyys,
Hys modyr clepede hym *Bewfys*,   20
    And no nothyr name ;
And hymself was full nys,
He ne axede naght, y wys,
    What he hyght, at hys dame.
As hyt befelle upon a day,
To wode he wente, on hys play,
    Of dere to have hys game ;
He fond a knyght whar he lay,
In armes that wer stout and gay,
    Isclayne, and made full tame.   30

That chyld dede of the knyghtes wede,
And anon he gan hym schrede,
    In that ryche armur ;
Whan he hadde do that dede,
To Glastynbery he yede,
    Ther ley the kyng Artour.

He knelede yn the halle,
Before the knyghtes alle,
    And grette hem with honour ;
And seyde, Kyng Artour, my lord,   40
Graunte me to speke a word,
    I pray the pur amour.

though Master Wace, not twenty years after the time of that unworthy prelate,
thus speaks of it :—
           " *Fist* Artur la ronde table,
             Dunt Breton *dient* meinte fable."

Than seyde Artour the kyng,
Anoon without any dwellyng,
  Tell me thyn name uplyght,
For sethen y was ybore,
Ne fond y me before
  Non so fayr of syght.

That chylde seyde, Be seynt Jame,
I not what ys my name,   50
  I am the more nys ;
But, whyle y was at hame,
My modyr, yn her game,
  Clepede me *Beau fyz.*
Than seyde Artour the kyng,
Thys ys a wonder thyng,
  Be god and seynt Denys,
Whanne he that wolde be a knyght,
Ne wat noght what he hyght,
  And ys so fayr of vys.   60

Now wyll y yeve hym a name,
Before yow alle yn same,
  For he ys so fayr and fre ;
Be god, and be seynt Jame,
So clepede hym never hys dame,
  What woman that so hyt be.
Now clepeth hym alle yn us
Lybeaux desconus.
  For the love of me ;*
Than may ye wete a row   70
The fayre unknowe,
  Sertes so hatte he.

---

* Giglan, the natural son of Gawain and the fairy *Blanchevallee,* appears at the court of king Arthur ; and, being asked his name, says that his mother (who had carefully concealed it) had never called him anything but *Beaufils;* in consequence of which the queen gives him that of *Le bel inconnu.* (*Histoire de Giglan,* n. d. 4to. g. l.) In this romance the lady is called Helen ; but the main incidents bear little or no resemblance to those of *Lybeaus.* See also the episode or adventure of *Beaumains,* in Sir Thomas Malory's *Mort d'Arthur.*

In the *Promptorium parvulorum* (Har. MS. 221) *Befyce* is explained *filius.*

Kyng Artour anon ryght
Made hym tho a knyght,
  In the selve day ;
And yaf hym armes bryght,
Hym gertte wyth swerde of myght,
  For sothe as y yow say.
And henge on hym a scheld,
Ryche and over geld   80
  Wyth a griffoun of say ;
And hym betok hys fader Gaweyn,
For to teche hym on the playne,
  Of ech knyghtes play.

Whan he was knyght imade,
Anon a bone there he bad,
  And seyde, My lord so fre,
In herte y were ryght glad,
That ferste fyghte yf y had,
  That ony man asketh the.   90
Thanne seyde Artour the kyng,
I grante the thyn askyng,
  What batayle that so hyt be ;
But me thyngeth thou art to ying,
For to done a good fyghtynge,
  Be awght that y can se.

Wythoute more resoun,
Duk, erl, and baroun,
  Whesch and yede to mete ;[*]

---

[*] It was a constant custom, in former times, to wash the hands before sitting down to, and after rising up from table. Thus, in *Emare*, *V.* 217 :—

    " Then the lordes that wer grete,
    They wesh and seten down to mete,
    And folk hem served swyde."

Again, V. 889 :—

    " Then the lordes, that wer grete,
    Wheschen ayeyn aftyr mete,
    And then com spycerye."

Again, in *Sir Orpheo*, V. 473 :—

    "The steward wasched and wente to mete."

Again, in *Le bone Florence of Rome*, V. 1009 :—

    " Then they wysche, and to mete be gone."

Thus, also, in *Robyn Hode and the potter*, the sheriff says—

    " Let os was, and go to mete."

Of all manere fusoun,　　　　　　　　100
As lordes of renoun,
　　Ynowgh they hadde ete.
Ne hadde Artour bote a whyle,
The mountance of a myle,
　　At hys table ysete,
Ther com a mayde ryde,
And a dwerk be here syde,
　　All beswette for hete.

That mayde was clepede Elene,
Gentyll, bryght, and schene,　　　　　110
　　A lady messenger;
Ther nas contesse, ne quene,
So semelych on to sene,
　　That myghte be her pere.
Sche was clodeth in Tars,
Rowmé and nodyng skars,
　　Pelvred wyth blauner;
Her sadell and her brydell, yn fere,
Full of dyamandys were,
　　Melk was her destrere.　　　　　　120

The dwerk was clodeth yn Ynde,
Before and ek behynde,
　　Stout he was and pert;
Among alle Crystene kende,
Swych on ne schold no man fynde,
　　Hys surcote was overt.
Hys berd was yelow as ony wax,
To hys gerdell henge the plex,
　　I dar well say yn certe;
Hys schon wer with gold ydyght,　　　130
And kopeth as a knyght,
　　That semede no povert.

Teandelayn was hys name,
Well swyde sprong hys fame,
　　Be north and be southe;
Myche he couthe of game,
With sytole, sautrye yn same,

F

Harpe, fydele and crouthe.
He was a noble dysour,
Wyth ladyes of valour,   140
   A mery man of mouthe ;
He spak to that mayde hende,
To telle thyn erynde,
   Tyme hyt were nouthe.

That mayde knelede yn halle,
Before the knyghtes * alle,
   And greet hem wyth honour,
And seyde, A cas ther ys yfalle,
Worse wythyn walle
   Was never non of dolour.   150
My lady of Synadowne
Is broght yn strong pryson,
   That ys greet of valour,
Sche prayd the sende her a knyght,
With herte good and lyght,
   To wynne her with honour.

Up start the yonge knyght,
Hys herte was good and lyght,
   And seyde, Artour, my lord,
I schall tho that fyght,   160
And wynne that lady bryght,
   Yef thou art trewe of word.
Than seyde Artour, That ys soth,
Certayn withoute noth,
   Thereto y bere record ;
God grante the grace and myght,
To holde up that lady ryghte,
   Wyth dente of thy sword.

Than gan Elene to chyde
And seyde, Alas that tyde   170
   That i was hyder ysent !
Thys word schall spryng * wyde,
Lord kyng now ys thy threde
   And thy manhod yschent.

---

  * Original reading : *knyzte.*   † Original reading : *spyng.*

Whan thou schalt sende a chyld
That ys wytles and wylde,
   To dele thoghty dent,
And hast knyghtes of mayn,
Launcelet, Perceval, and Gaweyn,
   Prys yn ech turnement. 180

Lybeaus desconus answerde *
Yet was y never aferde
   For doute of mannys awe,
To fyghte wyth spere or swerd,
Some dell y have ylerde,
   Ther many men were yslawe.
He that fleth for drede,
I wolde, be way or strete,
   Hys body wer to-drawe ;
I wyll the batayle take, 190
And never on forsake,
   As hyt ys Artours lawe.

Than seyde Artour anon ryght,
Thou getest none other knyght,
   Be god that boghte me dere,
Yef the thyngyth hym not wyght,†
Go gete the on wher thou myght,
   That be of more powere.
That mayde, for wreththe and hete,
Nolde neydyr drynke ne ete, 200
   For alle tho that ther were,
But satte down all thys mayd,
Tyll the table was ylayd,
   Sche and the dwerke yn fere.

Kyng Artour yn that stounde,
Hette of the table rounde,
   Four the beste knyhtes,
In armes hole and sounde,
The beste that myghte be founde,
   Arme Lybeaus anoon ryghtes. 210

---

* Original reading : *answerede.*
† Original reading : *Yef he thyngeth the not wyght..*

And seyde, thorgh helpe of Cryst,
That in the flome tok baptyste,
 He schall holde all hys heghtes, *
And be good champyoun
To the lady of Synadoun,
 And holde up alle her ryghtes.

To army thir knyghtes wer fayn,
The ferste was syr Gaweyn,
 That other syr Percevale,
The thyrthe syr Eweyn,†   220
The ferthde was syr Agrafrayn ;
 So seyth the Frenzsch tale.
They caste on hym a scherte of selk,
A gypell as whyte as melk,
 In that semely sale ;
And syght an hawberk bryght,
That rychely was adyght,
 Wyth mayles thykke and smale.

Gaweyn hys owene syre
Heng abowte hys swyre   230
 A scheld with a gryffoun,
And Launcelet hym broght a sper,
In werre with hym well to were,
 And also a fell fachoun.
And syr Oweyn hym broght a stede,
That was good at everych nede,
 And egre as lyoun,
And an helm of ryche atyre,
That was stele, and noon yre,
 Percevale sette on hys croun.   240

The knyght to hors gan spryng,
And rod to Artour the kyng,
 And seyde, My lord hende,
Yef me thy blessynge,
Anoon wythoute dwellynge,
 My wyll ys for to wende.

---

* Original reading : *hestes.*   † Original reading : *Gwèyn.*

Artour hys hond up haf,
And hys blessynge he hym yaf,
   As korteys kyng and hende ;
And seyde, God grante the grace,   250
And of spede space,
   To brynge the lady out of bende.

The mayde, stout and gay,
Lep on her palfray,
   The dwerk rod hyr besyde :
And tyll the thyrde day
Upon the knyght alwey
   Ever sche began chyde.
And seyde, Lorell and kaytyf,*
They thou wher worth swyche † fyfe,   260
   Ytynt now ys thy pryde ;
Thys pase before kepeth a knyght,
That wyth ech man wyll fyght,
   Hys name ys spronge wyde.

Wylleam Celebronche,
Hys fyght may no man staunch,
   He ys werrour so wyth ;
Thorugh herte, other thorugh honche,
Wyth hys sper he wyll launche
   All that ayens hym ryghtte.   270
Than seyd Lybeaus desconus,
Is hys feghtynge swych vys ?
   Was he never yhytte ?
Whatsoever me betyde,
To hym y wyll ryde,
   And loke how he sytte.

---

* Beaumains, in his expedition to relieve the Lady Liones, is treated in a similar manner by her sister Linet ; it is a very entertaining adventure. See *Mort d'Arthur*, P 1, C. 122, &c. See, also, that of the damsel *Maledisaunt*, and the young knight nicknamed *La cote male taild* P. 2, C. 44.

† Original reading : *swyr*.

Forth they ryden all thre,
Wyth merthe and greet solempnyte,
  Be a castell aunterous,
And the knyght they gon ysè,   280
Iarmeth bryght of ble,
  Up on the Vale perylous.
He bar a scheld of grene,
Wyth thre lyouns of gold schenc,
  Well prowde and precyous,
Of wych lengell and trappes
To dele ech man rappes
  Ever he was fous.

And whan he hadde of hem syght
To hem he rod full ryght,   290
  And seyde, Welcome, *beau frer*,
Ho that rydyght her day other nyght
Wyth me he mot take fyght,
  Other leve hys armes here.
Well, seyde Lybeaus desconus,
For love of swete Jhesus,
  Now let us passe skere ;
We haveth for to wende,
And beth fer from our frende,
  I and thys meyde yn fere.   300

Wylleam answerede tho,
Thou myght not skapy so,
  So god gef me good reste,
We wylleth er thou go
Fyghte bothe two
  A forlang her be-weste.
Than seyde Lybeaus, Now y se
That hyt nell non other be,
  In haste tho dy beste.
Thou take thy cours wyth schafte,   310
Ycf thou art knyght of crafte,
  For her es myn all preste.

No lengere they nolde abyde,
Togedere they gonne ryde,
   Wyth well greet randoun ;
Lybeaus desconus that tyde
Smot Wylleam yn the syde
   Wyth a sper feloun.
And Wylleam sat so faste,
That hys styropes to-braste,   320
   And hys hynder arsoun ;
Wylleam gan to stoupe
Mydde hys horses kroupe
   That he fell adoun.

Hys stede ran away,
Wylleam ne naght longe lay,
   But start up anoon ryght ;
And seyde, Be my fay,*
Before thys ylke day
   Ne fond y non so wyght.   330
Now my sted† ys ago,
Fyghte we a fote also,
   As thou art hendy knyght.
Tho seyde Lybeau desconus,
Be the love of Jhesus,
   Therto y am full lyght.

Togedere they gone spryng,
Fauchouns hy gonne out flyng,
   And foghte fell and faste ;
So harde they gonne drynge   340
That feer, without lesynge,
   Out of har helmes braste.
But Wylleam Selebraunche
Lybeau desconus gan lonche
   Thorghout that scheld yn haste,
A kantell fell to grounde,
Lybeau that ylke stounde
   In hys herte hyt kaste.

---

* Original reading : *lay.*   † Original reading : *iste.*

Thanne Lybeaus wys and whyght
Before hym as a noble knyght,   350
   As werrour queynte and sclegh,
Hawberk and krest yn fyght
He made fle doun ryght
   Of Wylleames helm and hegh.
And wyth the poynt of hys swerd
He schavede Wylleam ys berd,
   And com by flessch ryght neygh ;
Wylleam smot to hym tho,
That hys sword brast a-two,
   That many man hyt seygh.   360

Tho gan Wylleam to crye,
For love or Seynt Marye,
   Alyve let me passe ;
Hyt wer greet vylanye
To tho a knyght to deye
   Wepeneles yn place.
Than seyde Lybeaus desconus,
For love of swete Jhesus,
   Of lyve hast thou no grace,
But yef thou swere an oth,   370
Er than we two goth,
   Ryght her before my face.

In haste knele adoun,
And swer an my fachoun
   Thou schalt to Artour wende,
And sey, Lord of renoun,
As overcome and prysoun,
   A knyght me hyder gan sende.
That ys yclepede yn us
Lybeaus desconus,   380
   Unknowe of keth and kende.
Wylleam on knees doun sat,
And swor as he hym hat,
   Her forward word and ende.

Thus departede they alle,
Wyllyam to Artours halle
  Tok the ryghte way ;
As kas hyt began falle
Knyghtes proud yn palle
  He mette that selve day.   390
Hys susteres sones thre
Wher the knyghtes fre,
  That weren so stout and gay,
Whann they sawe Wyllyam blede,
As men that wolde awyede,
  They made greet deray :
And seyde, Eem Wylleam,
Ho hath doun the thys scham,
  That thou bledest so yerne ?
He seyde, Be seynt Jame,   400
On that naght to blame,
  A knyght stout and sterne.

A dwerk ryght her before,
Hys squyer as he wore,
  And ek a well fayr wyght ;
But othyng grevyth me sore,
That he hath do me swore,
  Upon hys fawchon bryght,
That y ne schall never more,
Tyll y come Artour before,   410
  Sojourne day ne nyght,
For prisoner i mot me yeld,
As overcome yn feld,
  Of hys owene knyght,
And never ayens hym bere
Nother scheld ne spere ;
  All this y have hym hyght.

Thanne seyde the knyghtes thre,
Thou schalt full well awreke be,
  For sothe wythout fayle ;   420
He alone ayens us thre
Nys naght worth a stre
  For to holde batayle.

G

Wend forth, eem, and do thyn othe.
And the traytour, be the rothe,
  We schull hym asayle ;
Right, be godes grace,
Ther he thys forest passe
  Thaugh he be dykke of mayle.

Now lete we Wylyam be,   430
That wente yn hys jornè,
  Toward Artour the kyng ;
Of these knyghtes thre
Hearkeneth, lordynges fre,
  A ferly fayr fyghtynge.
They armede hem full well,
Yn yren and yn stel,
  Wythout ony dwellyng,*
And leptede on stedes sterne,
And after gon yerne,   440
  To sle that knyght so yenge.

Herof wyste no wyght
Lybeaus the yonge knyght,
  But rod forth pas be pas ;
He and that mayde bryght
Togydere made all nyght
  Game and greet solas.
Mercy hy gan hym crye
That hy spak vylanye,
  He foryaf here that trespas.   450
De dwerke was her squyer,
And servede her fer and ner,
  Of all that nede was.

A morn, whan that hyt was day,
They wente yn har jornay
  Toward Synadowne,
Thanne saw they knyghtes thre,
In armes bryght of ble,
  Ryde out of Karlowne.

* Original reading : *Wellyng.*

All yärmed ynto the teth,   460
Everych swor hys deth,
  And stedes baye browne,
And cryde to hym full ryght,
Thef, turne agayn and fyght,
  Wyth the we denketh roune.

Lybeaus desconus tho kryde,
I am redy to ryde
  Ayens yow all ysame.
He prikede, as pryns yn pryde,
Hys stede yn bothe syde,   470
  In ernest and yn game.
The eldest brother gan bere
To syr Lybeaus a spere,
  Syr Gower was hys name,
But Lybeaus hym so nygh,
That he brak hys thegh,
  And ever efte he was lame.

The knyght gronede for payne,
Lybeaus wyth myght and mayne,
  Felde hym flat adownn;   480
The dwerk Teondeleyn
Tok the stede be the rayne,
  And lep ynto the arsoun:
And rod hym also sket
Ther that the mayde set,
  That was fayr of fasoun,
Tho lough that mayde bryght,
And seyde Thys yonge knyght,
  Ys chose for champyon.

The myddell brother com yerne,   490
Upon a stede sterne,
  Egre as lyoun,
Hym thoghte hys body wold berne,
But he myght also yerne
  Fell Lybeaus adoun.

As werrour out of wytte,
Lybeaus on helm he smyt,
    With a fell fachoun,
Hys strok so hard he set,
Thorgh helm and basnet,   500
    That sword tochede hys croun.

Tho was Lybeaus agreved,
Whan he feld on hedde
    That sword with egre mode,
Hys brond abowte he wevede,
All that he hyt he clevede,
    As werrour wyld and wode.
Allas, he seyde tho,
Oon ayens two
    To fyghte that ys good.   510
Wel faste they smyte to hym,
And he wyth strokes grym,
    Well harde ayens hem stode.

Tho sawe these knyghtes,
They ne hadde no myghtes
    To feghte ayens her fo.
To syr Lybeaus they gon up-yelde
Bothe har sperys and har schelde,
    And mercy cryde hym tho.

Lybeaus answerede, Nay,   520
The ne askapeth so away,
    Be god that schop mankende ;
Thou and thy brederen tway*
Schull plyght her your fay,
    To kyng Artour to wende ;
And sey, Lord of renounes,
As overcome and prysouns,
    A knyght us hyder gan sende,
To dwelle yn your bandown,†
And yelde you tour and toun,   530
    Ay wythouten ende.

---

* Original reading : *twayne*.   † Original reading : *bandwon*.

And but ye wyllen tho so
Sertes y schall you slo,
  Er than hyt be nyght ;
The knyghtes sweren tho
They wolde to Artour go,
  And trewes ther they plyght.
Thus departede day,
Lybeaus and that may,
  As they hadden tyght ;   540
Tyll the thyrde day
They ryde yn game and play,
  He and that mayde bryght :

And ever they ryden west,
In that wylde forest,
  Toward Synadowne ;
They nyste what ham was best
Taken they wolde reste,
  And myght not come to toun ;
A logge they dyghte of leves,   550
In the grene greves,
  With swordes bryght and broune ;
Therinne they dwellede all nyght,
He and that mayde bryght,
  That was so fayr of fasoun ;

And the dwerk gan wake,
For noo thef ne schuld take
  Har hors away with gyle ;
For drede he gan to quake,
For gret fer he sawe make   560
  Thannes half a myle.
Arys, he seyde, yong knyght,
To horse that thou wer ydyght.
  For dowte of peryle ;
For i here greet bost,

And fer smelle rost,
  Be god and seynt Gyle.
Lybeaus was stout and fer,
And lepte on hys destrer,
  Hente schelde and spere ;   570

And rod toward the fyer,
And whanne he nyghede ner,
   Two geauntes he saw ther.
That on was red and lothlych,
And that other swart as pych,
   Grysly bothe of chere ;
That oon held yn hys barme
A mayde yclepte yn hys arme,
   As bryght as blosle on brere.

The rede geaunt sterne   580
A wylde boor gan terne
   Abowte upon a spyte ;
That fyer bryght gan berne,
The mayde cryde yerne
   That som man schuld her ther wete :
And seyde, Wellaway !
That ever i bode thys day,
   With two fendes to sette !
Now help, Marie mylde,
For love of thy chylde,   590
   That y be naght foryette !

Than seyde Lybeaus, Be seynt Jame,
To save thys mayde fro schame
   Hyt wer a fayr apryse ;
To fyght with bothe yn same
Hyt wer no chyldes game,
   That beth so grymme and gryse.
He tok hys cours wyth schafte,
As knyght of kende crafte,
   And rod be ryght asyse ;   600
The blake geaunt he smot smert,
Thorgh the lyver, longe, and herte,
   That never he myghte aryse.

Tho flawe that mayde schene,
And thankede hevene quene,
   That swych socour her sente ;
Tho com that mayde Elene,
Sche and her dwerk y mene,
   And be the hond her hente ;

And ladde her ynto the greves,   610
Into that logge of leves,
  Wyth well good talent ;
And prayde swete Jhesus,
Helpe Lybeaus desconus,
  That he wer naght yschent.

The rede geaunt thore
Smot to Lybeaus wyth the bore,
  As man that wold awede ;
The strokes he sette so sore.
That hys cursere therfore,   620
  Deed to grounde yede.
Lybeaus was redy boun,
And lepte out of the arsoun,
  As sperk thogh out of glede ;
And egre as a lyoun,
He faught wyth hys fachoun,
  To quite the geauntes mede.

The geaunt ever faught,
And at the seconde draught,
  Hys spyte brak a two ;   630
A tre yn honde he kaught,
As a man that wer up-sawght
  To fyghte ayens hys fo.
And wyth the ende of the tre
He smot Lybeaus scheld a thre,
  And tho was Lybeaus well wo ;
And er he eft the tre up haf,
A strok Lybeaus hym yaf,
  Hys ryght arm fell hym fro.

The geaunt fell to grounde   640
Lybeaus that ylke stounde
  Smot of hys hedde ryght
Hym that he yaf er wounde
In that ylke stounde,
  He servede so aplyght.
He tok the heddes two,
And yaf hem the mayden tho,
  That he hadde fore that fyght ;

The mayde was glad and blythe,
And thonkede god fele syde   650
 That ever was he made knyght.

Then seyde Lybeaus, Gentyl dame,
Tell me what ys thy name,
 And wher thou wer ybore.
Sche seyde, Be seynt Jame,
My fader ys of ryche name,
 Woneth her before.
An erl, an hold hore knyght,
That hath be a man of myght,
 Hys name ys syr Autore ;   660
Men clepeth me Vyolette,
For me these geauntes besette
 Our castell full yore.

Yesterday yn the mornynge
Y wente on my playnge,
 And noon evell ne thoughte,
The geauntes, wythout lesynge,
Out of a kave gonne sprynge,
 And to thys fyer me brought.
Of hem y hedde ben yschent,   670
Ne god me socour hadde y sent,
 That all thys world wrought ;
He yeldede thys good dede
That for us gan blede,
 And wyth hys blod us bought.

Without ony more talkynge
To horse they gon sprynge,
 And ryde forth all yn same ;
He tolde the erl tydynge
How he wan yn fyghtynge   680
 Hys chyld fram wo and schame.
The two heddes wer ysent
Artour the kyng to present,
 With mochell gle and game ;
Thanne ferst yn court aros
Lybeaus desconus los,
 And hys gentyll fame.

The erl Autore also blyve
Profrede hys doftyr hym to wyve,
   Vyolette that may ;   690
And kasteles ten and fyve
And all after hys lyve
   Hys lond to have for ay.
Than seyde Lybeaus desconois,
Be the love of swete Jhesus,
   Naught wyve yet y ne may ;
I have for to wende
Wyth thys mayde so hende,
   And therefore have good day.

The erl, for hys good dede,   700
Yaf hym ryche wede,
   Scheld and armes brycht ;
And also a noble stede,
That doughty was of dede,
   In batayle and yn fyght.
They ryde forth all thre
Toward the fayre cytè,
   Kardevyle for soth hyt hyght ;
Thanne sawe they yn a park
A castell stout and stark,   710
   That ryally was adyght.

Swych saw they never non,
Imade of lyme and ston,
   Ikarneled all abowte ;
Oo, seyde Lybeaus, be seynt Jon,
Her wer a wordly won
   For man that wer yn dowte.
Tho logh that mayde bryght,
And seyde hyt owyth a knyght
   The beste her abowte ;   720
Ho that wyll wyth hym fyght,
Be hyt be day other nyght,
   He doth hym lowe lowte.

For love of hys lemman,
That ys so fayr a woman,
   He hath do crye and grede ;

H

Ho that bryngeth a fayryr oon,
A jerfaukon whyt as swan
   He schall have to mede.
Yef sche ys naght so bryght,   730
Wyth Gyfroun he mot fyght,
   And ye may not spede ;
Hys hed schall of be raft,
And sette upon a sper schaft,
   To se yn lengthe and brede.

And that thou mayst se full well
Ther stant yn ech a karnell
   An hed other two upryght ;
Than seyde Lybeaus also snell,
Be god and seynt Mychell,   740
   Wyth Gyffroun y schall fyght ;
And chalaunge the jerfawncon,
And sey that y have yn this toun,
   A lemman to so bryght ;
And yef he her wyll se,
I wyll hym schewy the,
   Be day other be nycht.

The dwerk seyde, Be Jhesus,
Gentyll Lybeaus desconus,
   That wer a greet peryle,   750
Syr Gyffroun le flowdous
In fyghtyng he hath an us
   Knyghtes to begyle.
Lybeaus answerede thar
Therof have thou no kar ;
   Be god and be seynt Gyle,
I woll ysè hys face
Er y westward pace
   From thys cyté a myle.

Wythoute a more resoune   760
They tok har [yn] the toune,
   And dwellede stylle yn pese ;
A morn Lybeaus was boun
For to wynne renoun,
   And ros, wythoute les :

And armede hym full sure,
In that selve armure
  That erl Autores was ;
Hys stede he began stryde,
The dwerk rod hym besyde,   770
  Toward that prowde palys.

Syr Gyffroun le fludous
Aros as was hys uus,
  In the morn-tyde ;
And whan he com out of hys hous,
He saw Lybeaus desconus
  Com prykynde as pryns yn pryde,
Wythoute a more abood
And ayens hym he rod,
  And thus to hym he cryde,   780
Wyth voys that was schrylle ; *
Comyst thou for good, other for ylle ?
  Tell me, and naght me hyde.

Than seyde Lybeaus al so tyte,
For y have greet delyte
  Wyth the for to fyght ;
For thou scyst greet despyte
That woman half so whyt,
  As thy lemman be ne myght ;
And y have on yn toune,   790
Fayryr of fassyoune,
  In clothes whan sche ys dyght ;
Therfore thy gerfawcoun
To Artour the kyng wyth kroun
  Bryng y schall wyth ryght.

Than seyde Gyfroun, Gentyll knyght,
How scholl we preve thys syght,
  Whych of hem fayrer be ?
Lybeaus answerede aplyght,
In Cardevyle cyté ryght,   800
  Ther ech man may hem se :

---

* Original reading : *schylle.*

And bothe they schull be sette
A myddes the market,
   To loke on bothe bond and fre ;
Yf my lemman ys broun,
To wynne the gerfawcoun
   Fyghte y wyll wyth the.

Than seyde Gyfroun, al so snell,
To all thys y graunte well,
   Thys day at underne-tyde ;   810
Be god and be seynt Mychell,
Out of thys castell
   To Karlof i schall ryde.
Har gloves up they held,
In forward as y teld,
   As princes prowde yn pryde ;
Syr Lybeaus al so snell
Rod hom to hys castell,
   No lenger* he nolde abyde ;

And commande mayde Elene,   820
As semelekest on to sene,
   Buske her and make her boun :
" I say, be hevene quene,
Gyffrouns lemman schene
   This day schall come to toun :
And bothe men you schall ysè,
A mydward the cytè,
   Both body and fasoun ;
Yef thou be naght so bryght,
Wyth Gyffroun i mot fyght,   830
   To wynne the Gerfaucoun."

Mayde Elene al so tyte,
In a robe of samyte
   Anoon sche gan her tyre,
To tho Lybeaus profyte
In kevechers whyt,
   Arayde wyth gold wyre.

---

* Original reading : *leng.*

A velvwet mantyll gay,
Pelvred wyth grys and gray,
  Sche caste abowte her swyre,   840
A sercle upon her molde,
Of stones and of golde,
  The best yn that enpyre.

Upon a pomely palfray
Lybeaus sette that may,
  And ryden forth all thre ;
Thanne ech man gan to say,
Her cometh a lady gay,
And semelych on to se.
Into the market sche rode,   850
And hovede and abode,
  A mydward the cytè ;
Than sygh they Gyffroun come ryde,
And two squyeres be hys syde,
  Wythout a more mayné.

He bar the scheld of goules,
Of sylver thre whyte oules,
  Of gold was the bordure,
Of the selve colours,
And of non other flowres,   860
  Was lyngell and trappure.
Hys squyer gan lede
Before hym upon a stede
  Thre schaftes good and sure ;
That other bar redy boun
The whyte gerfawcoun,
  That leyd was to wajour.

After hym com ryde
A lady proud yn pryde,
  Was clodeth yn purpel palle ;   870
That folk com fer and wyde
To se her bak and syde,
  How gentyll sche was and small.
Her mantyll was rosyne,
Pelvred with ermyne,
  Well ryche and reall ;

A sercle upon her molde,
Of stones and of golde,
   Wyth many a juall.

As the rose her robe was red,   880
The her sehon on hyr heed,
   As gold wyre schyneth bryght;
Ayder browe as selken threde,
Abowte yn lengthe and yn brede,
   Hyr nose was strath and ryght.
Her eyen gray as glas,
Melk-whyt was her * face,
   So seyde that her sygh wyth syght;
Her swere long and small,
Her beawte telle all   890
   No man wyth mouth ne myght.

Togedere men gon hem bryng
A mydward the chepyng,
   Har beawte to dyscrye;
They seyde, olde and yenge,
For soth wythoute lesyng,
   Betwene hem was partye.
Gyffrouns lemman ys clere
As ys the rose yn erbere,
   For soth and naght to lye;   900
And Elene, the messengere,
Semeth but a lavendere
   Of her norserye.

Than seyde Gyffroun le fludous,
Syr Lybeaus desconus,
   Thys hauk thou hast forlore;
Than seyde Lybeaus desconus,
Nay swhych nas never myn uus,
   Justy y well therfore.
And yef thou berest me doun,   910
Tak my heed the fawkoun,
   As forward was before;

---

* Original reading : *he.*

And yf y bere doun the,
The hauk schall wende wyth me,
  Maugre thyn heed hore :
What help mo tales telld?
They ryden yn to the feld,
  And wyth ham greet partye ;
Wyth coronals stef and stelde,
Eyther smyt other in the schelde,   920
  Wyth greet envye.
Har saftes breke asonder,
Har dentes ferthe as thonder,
  That cometh out of the skye ;
Taborus and trompours,
Herawdes goode descoverours,*
  Har strokes gon descrye.

Syr Gyffroun gan to speke,
Breng a schaft that nell naght breke,
  A schaft wyth a cornall ;   930
Thys yonge ferly frek
Ys yn hys sadell steke,
  As stone yn castell wall.
Thaugh he wer whyght werrour,
As Alysander, other Artour,
  Launcelot, other Percevale,
I wyll do hym stoupe
Over hys horses croupe,
  And yeve hym evele fall.

The knyghtes bothe two,   940
Togydere they ryden tho,
  With well greet raundoun ;
Lybeaus smot Gyffroun so,
That hys scheld fell hym fro,
  In that feld adoun.
The lough all that ther wes,
And seyde wythoute les,
  Duke, erl, and baroun,
That yet never they ne seygh
Man that myghte dreygh   950
  To justy wyth Gyffroun.

* Original reading : *descoverous.*

Gyffroun hys hors outryt,
And was wode out of wyt,
   For he myghte naght spede ;
He rod agayn as tyd,
And Lybeaus so he smyt,
   As man that wold awede.
But Lybeaus sat so faste,
That Gyffroun doun he caste,
   Bothe hym and hys stede ;   960
Gyffrounys legge * to-brak,
That men herde the krak,
   Aboute yn lengthe and brede.

Tho seyde all tho that ther wore,
That Gyffroun hadde forlore,
   The whyte gerfawkoun ;
To Lybeaus thay hym bore,
And wente, lasse and more,
   Wyth hym ynto the toune.
Syr Gyffroun, upon hys scheld,   970
Was ybore hom fram the feld,
   Wyth care and rufull roun ;
The gerfawkoun ysent was,
Be a knyght that hyght Gludas,
   To Artour kyng wyth kroun.

And wryten all the dede
Wyth hym he gan lede,
   The hauk how that he wan ;
Tho Artour herde hyt rede,
To hys knyghtes he seyde,   980
   Lybeaus well werry-kan.
He hath me sent the valour
Of noble dedes four
   Sethe he ferst began ;
Now wyll y sende hym tresour,
To spendy wyth honour,
   As falleth for swych a man.

And hundred pound honest
Of floryns wyth the best
   He sente to Cardelof than ;   990

---

* Original reading : *regge.*

Tho Lybeaus helde hys feste,
That fourty dayes leste,
   Of lordes of renoun.
Than Lybeaus and that may
Token hyr ryghte way
   Toward Synadowne.
And fayre her leve token thay,
To wende ynto another contray,
   Of duk, erl and baroun ;
As they ryden an a lowe,   1000
Hornes herde they blowe,
   Ther unther the doune ;

And houndes ronne greet and smale,
Hontes grette yn the vale
   The dwerke seyde that drowe
For to telle soth my tale,
Fele yeres ferely fale
   That horn well y thede knowe.
Hym blowyth syr Otes de Lyle,
That servede my lady som whyle,   1010
   In her semyly sale,
Whanne he was take wyth gyle
He flawe for greet peryle
   West ynto Wyrhale.

As they ryde talkynge
A rach ther come flyngynge
   Overtwert the way,
Thanne seyde old and yynge, *
From her ferst gynnynge,
   They ne sawe hond never so gay.   1020
He was of all colours
That man may se of flours,
   Betwene Mydsomer and May ;
That mayde sayde al so snell,
Ne saw y never no juell
   So lykynge to my pay :

---

* Original reading : *Yngc.*

1

God wold that y hym aughte!
Lybeaus anoon hym kaghte,
　　And yaf hym to mayde Elene;
They ryden forth all yn saght,　　　　　　1030
And tolde how knyghtes faght,
　　For ladyes bryght and schene.
Ne hadde they ryde but a whyle,
The mountance of a myle,
　　In that forest grene,
They sawe an hynde com styke,
And two grehoundes ylyke,
　　Be that rech that y er of mene.

They hovede unther a lynde,
To se the cours of the hynde,　　　　　　1040
　　Lybeaus and hys fere;
Thanne seygh they come byhynde
A knyght iclodeth yn* Ynde,
　　Upon a bay destrere.
Hys bugle he gan to blowe,
For hys folk hyt schuld knowe
　　In what stede he wer;
He seyde to hem that throwe,
Syr, that rach was myn owe,
　　Ygon for sevene yere:　　　　　　1050

Frendes, leteth hym go.
Lybeaus answerede tho,
　　That schall never betyde,
For wyth myn handes two
I hym yaf that mayde me fro
　　That hoveth me besyde.
Tho seyde ser Otes de Lyle,
Than artow yn peryle,
　　Byker yef thou abyde.
Tho seyde Lybeaus, Be seynt Gyle,　　　　1060
I ne yeve naght of thy gyle,
　　Cherll, though thou chyde.

---

* Original reading : *y.*

Then seyde syr Otes de Lyle,
Syr, thyn wordes beth fyle,
  Cherll was never my name ;
My fader an erll was whyle,
The countesse of Karlyle
  Certes was my dame.
Wer ych yärmed now,
Redy as art thou,   1070
  We wolde feyghte yn same ;
But thou the rach me leve,
Thou pleyyst, er hyt be eve,
  A wonder wylde game.

Tho seyde Lybeaus also prest,
Therof tho thy best,
  Thys rach schall wyth me wende.
They tok har way ryght west,
In that wylde forest,
  Ryght as the dwerk hem kende.   1080
The lord wyth greet errour
Rod hom to hys tour,
  And after hys frendes sende,
And tolde hem anon ryghtes
That on of Artourys knyghtes
  Schamelych gan hym schende ;

And hadde hys rach ynome.
Thanne seyde alle and some,
  The traytour schall be take,
And never ayen hom come,   1090
Thaugh he wer thoghtyer gome,
  Than Launcelet du Lake.
Tho dyghte they hem all to armes,
Wyth swerdes and wyth gysarmes,
  As werre schold awake ;
Knytes and squyeres,
Lepte on her destrerys,
  For har lordes sake.

Upon an hell well hyghe
Lybeaus ther they syghe,   1100
  He rod pas be pas ;

To hym they gon crye,
Traytour, thou schalt dye,
    For thy wykkede trespas.
Syr Lybeaus ayen beheld
How fulfelde was the feld,
    So greet peple ther was;
He seyde, Mayde Elene,
For our rach, y wene,
    Us cometh a karfull cas.   1110

I rede that ye drawe
Into the wode schawe,
    Your heddes for to hyde;
For I am swyde fawe,
Thaugh ych schulde be slawe,
    Bykere of hem y woll abyde.
Into the wode they rode,
And Lybeaus theroute abothe,
    As aunterous knyght yn pryde;
Wyth bowe, and wyth arblaste,   1120
To hym they schote faste,
    And made hym woundes wyde.

Lybeaus stede ran,
And bar doun hors and man,
    For nothyng nolde he* spare;
That peple seyde than,
Thys ys fend Satan,
    That mankende wyll forfare.
For wham Lybeaus arafte
After hys ferste drawghte   1130
    He slep for evermare:
But sone he was besette
As theer ys yn a nette
    Wyth grymly wondes sare.

Twelf knyghtes all prest
He saw come yn the forest,
    In armes cler and bryght;

---

* Original reading: *her*.

Al day they hadde yrest,
And thought* yn that forest,
 To sle Lybeaus the knyght.   1140
Of sute were all twelfe,
That on was the lord hymselfe,
 In ryme to rede aryght ;
They smyte to hym all at ones,
And thoghte to breke hys bones,
 And felle hym doun yn fyght.

Tho myghte men her dynge,
And swordes lowde rynge,
 Among hem all yn fere ;
So harde they gonne thrynge,   1150
The sparkes gonne out sprynge,
 Fram scheld and helmes clere.
Lybeaus slough of hem thre,
And the fourth gonne to fle,
 And thorst naght nyghhe hym nere,
The lord dwellede yn that schour,
And hys sones four,
 To selle har lyves there.

Ther roune tho rappes ryve,
He ayens hem fyve,   1160
 Faught as he were wod ;
Neygh doun they gonne hym dryve,
As water doth of clyve,
 Of hym ran the blode.
As he was neygh yspylt,
Hys swerd brast yn the hylt,
 Tho was he mad of mode ;
The lord a strok hym sette,
Through † helm and basnette,
 That yn the scheld hyt stode.   1170

Aswogh he fell adoun,
And hys hynder arsoun,
 As man that was mate ;

---

* Original reading : *though.*   † Original reading : *though.*

Hys fomen were well boun,
To perce hys acketoun,
  Gypell, mayl, and plate.
As he gan sore smerte,
Up he pullede hys herte,
  And keverede of hys state;
An ex he hente all boun,   1180
At hys hynder arsoun,
  Allmest hym thoughte to late.

Than besterede he hym as a knygth,
Thre stedes heoddes doun ryght,
  He smot at strokes thre;
The lord saw that syght,
And on hys courser lyght,
  Awey he gan to fle,
Lybeaus no lenger abode,
But aftyr hym he rode,   1190
  And unther a chesteyn tre,
Ther he hadde hym quelthe,
But the lord hym yelde,
  At hys wylle to be.

And be sertayne extente
Tresour, lond, and rente,
  Castell, halle, and bour,
Lybeaus therto consente
In forward * that he wente
  To the kyng Artour,   1200
And seye, Lord of renoun,
As overcome and prysoun
  Y am to thyne honour.
The lord grauntede to hys wylle
Bothe lowthe and stylle,
  And ledde hym to hys bour.

Anoon that mayde Elene,
Wyth gentyll men fyftene
  Was fet to that castell

† Original reading : *soward.*

Sche and the dwerke bydene   1210
Tolde dedes kene
   Of Lybeaus how hyt fell.
Swyche presentes four
He hadde ysent kyng Artour,
   That he wan fayr and well ;
The lord was glad and blythe,
And thonketh fele syde
   God and seynt Mychell.

Now reste we her awhyle
Of syr Otes de Lyle,   1220
   And telle we other tales.
Lybeaus rod many a myle,
Among aventurus fyle,
   In Yrland and yn Wales.
Hyt befell yn the month of June,   *1225*
Whan the fenell hangeth yn toun,
   Grene yn semely sales,
Thys somerys day ys long,
Mery ys the fowles song,
   As * notes of the nyghtyngales.   1230

That tyme Lybeaus com ryde,
Be a ryver syde,
   And saw a greet cytè,
Wyth palys prowd yn pryde,
And castelles heygh and wyde,   *1235*
   Wyth gates greet plentè.
He axede what hyt hyght.
The mayde seyde anon ryght,
   Syr, y telle hyt the,
Men clepeth hyt Yledor,†   1240
Her hath be fyghtynge more
   Thanne owher yn any countrè.

For a lady of prys,
Wyth rode rede as rose on ryse,
   Thys countre ys yn dowte ;   *1245*

---

* Original reading: *A.*
† *L'isle d'or*, the Isle of Gold, or Golden Island ; but whether designed for French or English seems rather doubtful.

A geaunt hatte Maugys,
Nowher hys per ther nys,
   Her hathe be leyde abowte.
He ys blak as ony pych.
Nower ther ys non swych,   1250
   Of dede sterne and stoute ;
Ho that passeth the bregge
Hys armes he mot legge,
   And to the geaunt alowte.

Tho seyde Lybeaus, Mayde hende,
Schold y wonde to wende,
   For hys dentys ille ;
Yf god me grace sende,
Er thys day come to ende,
   Wyth fyght y schall hym spylle.   1260
I have yseyn grete okes
Falle for wyndes strokes,
   The smale han stonde stylle ;
They y be yyng and lyte,
To hym yyt wyll y smyte
   Do god all hys wylle.

They ryden forth all thre
Toward that fayre cytè,
   Me clepeth hyt Ylledore ;
Maugeys they gonne ysè   1270
Upon the bregge of tre,
   Bold as wylde bore.
Hys scheld as blakke as pych,
Lyngell armes trappur was swych,
   Thre mammettes therynne wore,
Of gold gaylyth ygeld,
A schafte an honde he held,
   And oo scheld hym before.

He cryde to hym yn despyte,
Say, thou felaw yn whyt,   1280
   Tell me what art thou,
Torne hom agayn all so tyt,
For thy owene profyt,
   Yef thou lovede thy prow.

Lybeaus seyde anoon ryght,
Artour made me knyght,
  To hym i made a vow,
That y ne schulde never turne bak,
Therfore, thou devell yn blak,
  Make the redy now.   1290

Syr Lybeaus and Maugys,
On stedes prowde of prys,
  Togedere ryde full ryght ;
Bothe lardes and ladyes
Leyn out yn pomet touris *
  To se that sely fyght ;
And prayde wyth good wyll,
Bothe lode and styll,
  Helpe Lybeaus the knyght ;
And that fyle geaunt,   1300
That levede yn Termagaunt,†
  That day to deye yn fyght.

---

* Original reading : *tours*. The poet certainly intended a rhyme, if ever so bad.

† So, afterward, in the *King of Tars :*—

  " Of *Tirmagaunt* and of *Mahoun*."

" Termagaunt," says Dr. Percy, " is the name given in the old romances to the god of the Saracens : in which he is constantly linked with Mahound or Mahomet." (i, 76.) " This word," he adds, " is derived by the very learned editor of Junius from the Anglo-Saxon Tyr, very, and Mazan, mighty. As this word had so sublime a derivation, and was so applicable to the true god, how shall we account for its being so degraded ? Perhaps Tyr-mazan or *Termagant* had been a name originally given to some Saxon idol, before our ancestors were converted to christianity ; or had been the peculiar attribute of one of their false deities ; and therefore the first christian missionaries rejected it as profane and improper to be implied [*r*. applied] to the true god. Afterwards, when the irruptions of the Saracens into Europe, and the Crusades into the east, had brought them acquainted with a new species of unbelievers, our ignorant ancestors, who thought all that did not receive the christian law were necessarily pagans and idolaters, supposed the Mahometan creed was in all respects the same with that of their pagan forefathers, and therefore made no scruple to give the ancient name of *Termagant* to the god of the Saracens : just in the same manner as they afterwards used the name of *Sarazen* to express any kind of pagan idolater." (77.) " I cannot," says he, afterward, " conclude this short memoir, without observing that the French romancers, who had borrowed the word Termagant from us, and applied it as we in their old romances, corrupted it into Tervagaunte. This may be added to the other proofs adduced in these volumes of the great intercourse that formerly sub-

K

> Har scheldes brooke asonder,
> Har dentes ferd as donder,
>   The peces gonne out sprynge ;
> Ech man hadde wonder
> That Lybeaus ne hadde ybe unther,
>   At the ferst gynnyng.

sisted between the old minstrels and legendary writers of both nations, and that they mutually borrowed each others romances " (78.) In a note, at p. 379, he, likewise observes that "the old French romancers, who had corrupted TERMAGANT into TERVAGANT, couple it with the name of Mahomet as constantly as ours. As TERMAGANT," he says, "is evidently of Anglo-Saxon derivation, and can only be explained from the elements of that language, its being corrupted by the old French romancers proves that they borrowed some things from ours." In another note (III., xxii), in order to support his hypothesis, that " The stories of king Arthur and his round table, of Guy and Bevis, with some others, were probably the invention of English minstrels," he has the following words: "That the French romancers borrowed some things from the English, appears from the word TERMAGANT, which they took up from our minstrels, and corrupted into TERVAGAUNTE. . . . What is singular, Chaucer, who was most conversant with the French poets, adopts their corruption of this word.—See TYRWHITT's EDIT."

In this pursuit the venerable prelate (though he might not be one at that time) has suffered himself to be misled by an *ignis fatuus*. All that he has said, about Tyr-Mazan, or *Termagant* being the name of a Saxon deity, remains to be proved. The learned editor of Junius imposed upon him : the combination Tyr Mazan, is not to be found even in his own Saxon dictionary, neither, according to that authority, is Tyr, very ; and maza, not mazan, is mighty : and, after all, this is only in effect the *ter-magnus* of former etymologists. As little foundation is there for supposing that the French romancers not only borrowed the word *Termagant* from the English, but, likewise, corrupted it into TERVAGAUNTE : which is contrary to every authenticated fact. The English romancers not only servilely followed the French, but even themselves corrupted the word TERVAGANTE, after they had got it. This corruption, however, must have taken place before the time of Chaucer, who, notwithstanding what Dr. P. has asserted, even in Mr. Tyrwhitt's edition, gives the English corruption, and not the French original :—

> " He sayde, Child, by TERMAGAUNT."

(II. 235 ; and see IV., 318.)

A much greater mistake than the present editor made, by inadvertently quoting his own book, by which the worthy doctor (forgetful of his own hallucinations) was pleased to say "all confidence [had] been destroyed."

But, in the *King of Tars*, a romance, in all probability, anterior to Chaucer's time, as preserved in the Edinburgh MS. we find—

> "Be Mahoun and TERVAGANT : "

and had we more copies of that age, we should, doubtless, recover many other instances of the word ; as, in fact, there may be in that identical MS.

With respect to the etymology of the original name TERVAGANTE (for it is perfectly ridiculous to seek for that of the corruption *Termagant*), it may, possibly, be referred to the two Latin words *ter* and *vagans*, i.e., the action of going

Thanne drough dey swordes bothe,
As men that weren wrothe,   1310
· And gonne togedere dynge ;
Lybeaus smot Maugys so,
That hys scheld fell hym fro,
And yn to the feld gan flynge.

Maugys was queynte and quede,
And smot of the stedes heed,
That all fell out the braynce ;

or turning thrice round, a very ancient ceremony in magical incantation. Thus Medea, in Ovid's *Metamorphosis* (L. 7, V. 189):—

> " *Ter se convertit ; ter sumtis flumine crinem*
> *Irroravit aquis ; ternis ululatibus ora*
> *Solvit.*"

> " She turned her thrice about, as oft she thr ew
> On her pale tresses the nocturnal dew,
> Then yelling thrice, &c."

Vago, indeed, in pure Latin, means to wander, but, in barbarous times, the classical sense of a word was not much regarded : of this, however, one cannot be confident. Tir, or Tyr, in Saxon, and the ancient Cimbric, was the name of Odin, or some other northern deity, and, metonymically, any great leader, prince, lord, or emperor ; and is occasionally applied, in composition, to God, the Creator. See Lye's Dictionary, and Hickes's *Thesaurus*. But, admitting *Tervagante* or *Termagant* to have some connection with the Saxon or Cimbric term, it will, by no means, prove that we did not obtain the word from the French, whose language, every one knows, was as much a dialect of the ancient Cimbric as that of the Anglo-Saxon. The word *three* had some mystic signification with the ancients :—

> " *Tergeminamque Hecaten, tria virginis ora Dianæ.*"   Vir. Æ. IV.

Termagant, therefore, has been corrupted, by the English, from *Tervagant*, precisely in the same manner as we have corrupted *cormorant* from *corvorant*, and *malmsey* from *malvesie*. The Italian poets have it *Trivigante*. Thus Ariosto :—

> " *Bestemmiando Macone,* e 'Trivigante."

It, likewise, occurs in the *Gierusalemme liberata* of Tasso. They, too, doubtless, were indebted for it to the French.

•*• King Herod, in the Coventry *Corpus Christi* play, constantly swears by Mahomet, but never by Termagant. So in fo. 173 :

> " Now be Mahound, my god of grace."

One of the soldiers, who are set to watch the sepulchre, calls him " Seynt Mahownde."

" *Tervagant, l'un des dieux prétendus des Mahométans*," is a character in "*Le jeu de S. Nicolas*," a very ancient French mystery (see *Fabliaux ou contes*, II., 131) ; but no such personage, or even name, occurs in any English mystery or morality now extant, or of which we have any account ; though, from the following passage, in Bale's *Acts of English Votaries*, it would seem that some such character had, in his time, been known to the stage :—

> " Grennyng upon her, lyke *Termagauntes* in a play."

The stede fell doune deed,
Lybeaus nothyng ne sede,
   Bot start hym up agayn.   1320
An ax he hente boun,
That heng at hys arsoun,
   And smot a strok of mayn ;
Thorugh Maugys stedes swyre,
And forkarf bon and lyre,
   That heed fell yn the playn.

Afote they gonne to fyghte,
As men that wer of myghte,
   The strokes betwene hem two
Descryve no man ne myghte,   1330
For they wer unsyght,
   And eyder othres fo.
Fram the our of pryme*
Tyll hyt was evesong tyme
   To fyghte they wer well thrɔ ;   1335
Syr Lybeaus durstede sore,
   And seyde Maugys thyn ore,†
      To drynke lette me go :

---

   * It was customary with the Christian kings, knights, and soldiers, to cease fighting at evensong or vespers, observed at six o'clock. Thus, in the ancient Catalan romance of *Tirant lo Blanch.* Barcelona, 1497, folio, it is said, " *E continuant tostemps la batailla era ja quasi hora* de vespres, &c. So, likewise, in the *Histoire de Guerin de Montglave,* Lyons, 1585, 8vo, " *& maintint la guerre* jusques à l'heure de vespres." In the old Ballad of *The Hunts of Cheviat :*—

       " When even-song bell was rang, the battell was nat half done ;"

and it became sinful, of course, to fight any longer. The same circumstance is thus noticed in the more modern ballad of *Chevy-Chase :*—

       " The fight did last, from break of day,
          Till setting of the sun ;
       For, when they rung the evening-bell,
          The battle scarce was done."

Dr. Percy has confounded the *vesper bell* with the *curfew.* The reason of this temporary cessation of bloodshed, proceeded from respect to the Virgin Mary ; for, at this hour, the angelical salutation was sung ; whence it was sometimes called the *Ave Maria* bell. It is still customary, upon the Spanish stage, for the actors, in the midst of the grossest and most indecent buffoonery, to fall down on their knees, and pull out their beads, at the sound of this bell.

   † Thus, in Chaucer's *Millere's Tale, V.* 3724 :
       " Lemman, thy grace, and, swete bird, *thyn ore.*"
In the learned editor's note on this passage he explains *ore* to signify " *grace,*

And y schall graunte the
What bone thou byddest me,   1340
   Swych cas yef that be tyt ;
Greet schame hyt wold be
For durste a knyght to sle, ~
   And no mare profyt.
Maugys grauntede hys wyll,   1345
To drynke all hys fyll,
   Wythout any despyte ;
As Lybeaus ley on the bank,
And thorugh hes helm he drank,
   Maugys a strok hym smyt.   1350

That yn the ryuer he fell,
Hys armes echadell,
   Was weet and evell adyght ;
But up he start snell,
And seyde, Be seynt Mychell,   1355
   Now am y two so lyght.
What wendest thou, fendes fere ?
Uncrystenede that were
   Tyll y saw the wyth syght ;
I schall for thys baptyse   1360
Ryght well quyte thy servyse,
   Thorugh grace of god almight.

---

favour, protection:" and cites, as 'an additional instance, in support of that explana-
tion, the present text, " where," he says, "*thyne ore* must be understood to mean
with thy favour, as in this passage of Chaucer."

The same phrase occurs frequently in *Syr Bevys,* though not precisely, at least, in
every instance, with Mr. Tyrwhitt's signification :—

     " She saide, Bevys, lemman, *thyn ore,*
      Thou art wounded wonder sor:."
     " Mercy, saide Bradmodde, *thyn ore.*"
     " There is no man, by goddys *ore.*"
     " Then sayd Bevys, for Crystes *ore.*"

Thus, likewise, Robert of Gloucester, P. 39 :—

     " The maister fel adoun on kne, and criede *mercy* and *ore.*"

Again :—

     " Therfore the erl of Kent he bysought *milc* and *ore.*"

Again, in *The erl of Toulous,* V. 583 :—

     " Y aske *mercy* for goddys *ore.*"

Thanne newe fyght they began,
Eyther tyll other ran,
   And delede dentes strong ;
Many a gentylman,
And ladyes whyt as swan,
   For Lybeaus handes wrong.
For Maugys yn the feld
Forkarf Lybeaus scheld,   1370
   Wyth dente of armes long ;
Thanne Lybeaus ran away,
Ther that Maugys scheld lay,
   And up he gan hyt fonge.

And ran agayn to hym
Wyth strokes stout and grym,
   Togydere they gonne asayle,
Besyde that ryver brym
Tyll hyt darkede dym
   Betwene hem was batayle.   1380
Lybeaus was werrour wyght,
And smot a strok of myght,
   Thorugh gypell, plate, and mayll ;
Forthwyth the scholder bon
Maugys arm fyll of anoon,
   Into the feld saunz fayle.

The geaunt thys gan se
Islawe that he schulde be,
   And flaugh wyth myght and mayn.
Lybeaus after gan fle,   1390
Wyth sterne strokes thre,
   And smot hys back atweyn.
The geaunt ther beleveth
Lybeaus smot of hys heved,
   And of the batayle was fayn.   1395
He wente ynto the toun
Wyth fayr processioun,
   That folk com hym agayn.

A lady, whyt as flowr,
That hyghte *la dame d'amore*,   1400
   A feng hym fayr and well ;

And thankede hys honour,
That he was her socour,
   Ayens the geaunt so fell.
To chambre sche gan hym lede,
And dede of all hys wede,
   And clodede hym yn pell ;
And proferede hym wyth word
For to be her lord,
   In cyté and castell.   1410

Lybeaus grauntede yn haste,
And love to her he caste,
   For sche was bryght and schene ;
Alas he ne hadde ybe chast !
For aftyrward at last,
   Sche dede hym greet tene.
For twelf monthe and more
Lybeaus dwellede thore,
   And mayde Elene ;
That never he myghte out-breke,   1420
For to help a wreke
   Of Synadowne the quene.

For thys fayr lady*
Kowthe moch of sorcery,
   More then other wycches fyfe ;   1425
Sche made hym melodye,
Of all manere menstracy,
   That man myghte descryve.
Whan he seygh her face,
Hym thought he was   1430
   In Paradys alyve ;
Wyth fantasme, and fayrye,
Thus sche blerede hys yye,
   That evell mot sche thryve.

Tyll hyt fell on a day,   1435
He mette Elene that may,
   Wythinne the castell tour ;

---

* This lady bears a strong resemblance to the no less magical than beauteous fairies, the Calypso of Homer, and the Alcina of Ariosto ; both of whom deluded and detained Ulysses and Rogero in the manner *la dame d'amour* here treats Lybeaus.

To hym sche gan to say,
Syr knyght, thou art fals of fay,
   Ayens the king Artour.   1440
For love of a woman,
That of sorcery kan,
   Thou doost greet dyshonour ;
The lady of Synadowne
Longe lyght in prisoun,
   And that is greet dolour.

Lybeaus herd her so speke,
Hym thought hys hert wold breke,
   For sorow and for schame ;
And at a posterne unsteke   1450
Lybeaus gan out-breke
   Fram that gentyll dame ;
And tok wyth hym hys stede,
Hys scheld, and hys ryche wede,
   And ryde forth all ysame ;
Her styward stout and sterne,
He made hys squyere,
   Gyfflet was hys name :

And ryde, as fast as they may,
Forth yn her jornay,   1460
   On stedes bay and browne ;
Upon the thyrdde thay
They saw a cyté gay,
   Me clepeth hyt Synadowne.
Wyth castell heygh and wyde,
And palys prowd yn pryde,
   Werk of fayr fassoune ;
But Lybeaus desconus
He hadde wonder of an uus
   That he saw do yn toune.   1470

For gore, and fen, and full wast,
That was out ykast,
   Togydere they gaderede y wys ;
Lybeaus axede yn hast,
Tell me, mayde chast,
   What amounteth thys.

They taketh all that hore,
That er was out ybore,
   Me thyngeth they don a mys.
Thanne seyde mayde Elene,   1480
Syr, wythouten wene,
   I schalle the telle how yt ys.

No knyght for nessche ne hard,
They he schold be forfard,
   Ne geteth her non ostell,
For love of a styward,
Men clepeth hym syr Lambard,
   Constable of thys castell.
Ryde to that est gate,
And axede thyn in therate,   1490
   Bothe fayre and well ;
And er he bete thy nede,
Justes he wyll the bede,
   By god and seynt Mychell.

And yf he beryth the doun,
Hys trompys schull be boun,
   Har bemes for to blowe ;
And thorughout Synadowne,
Bothe maydenes, and garssoun,
   Fowyll fen schull on the throwe :   1500
And thanne to thy lyves ende,
In whett stede that thow wende,
   For coward werst thou knowe,
And thus may kyng Artour
Lese hys honour,
   Thorugh thy dede slowe.

Than seyde Lybeaus al so tyt,
That wer a greet dyspyt,
   For any man alyve ;
To tho Artour profyt,   1510
And make the lady quyt,
   To hym y wyll dryve.
Syr Gyfflette, make the yare !—
Thyder we wyllyth fare,
   Hastely and blyve.

                I.

They ryde thy ryght gate,
Even to the castell-yate,
  Wyth fayre schaftes fyfe.

And at the fayr castell
They axede her ostell,   1520
  For aunterous knyghtes ;
The porter, fayre and well,
Lette ham yn al so snell,
  And axede anon ryghtes :
Ho ys yowre governowre ?
They seyde, Kyng Artour,
  That ys man most of myghtes ;
And welle of curtesye,
And flowr of chyvalrye,
  To felle hys son yn fyghtes.   1530

The porter profytable,
To hys lord the constable
  Thus hys tale tolde,
And wythoute fable,
Syr, of the rownde table
  Beth come knyghtes bolde ;
That beth armed sure,
In rose-reed armure,
  Wyth thre lyouns of gold ;
Lambard therof was fayn,   1540
And swore oth certayn.
  Wyth hem juste he wolde.

And bad hem make yare,
Into the feld to fare,
  Wythoute the castell gate ;
The porter nold naght spare,
As grehound doth the hare,
   To ham he ran full wate
And seyde anon ryghtes,
Ye aunterous knyghtes,   1550
  For nothyng ye ne late ;
Loketh your scheldes be strong,
Your schaftes good and long,
  Your saket and faunplate.

And rydeth ynto the feld,
My lord, wyth sper and scheld,
   Cometh wyth yow to play.
Lybeaus spak wordes bold,
That ys a tale ytold,
   Well lykynge unto my pay.   1560
Into the felde they ryde,
And hovede and abyde,
   As best broght to bay ;
The lord of sente hys stede,
Hys scheld, hys ryche wede,
   Hys atyre was stout and gay.

Hys scheld was of gold fyn,
The bores heddes therinne,
   As blak as brond ybrent ;
The bordur of ermyne,   1570
Nas non so queynte of gyn,
   From Karlell ynto Kent.
And of the same paynture
Was lyngell and trappure
   Iwroght well fayre and gent ;
Hys schaft was strong wythall,
Theron a stef coronall,
   To dely doghty dent.

And whane that stout styward,
That hyghte syr Lambard,   1580
   Was armede at all ryghtes,
He rood to the feld ward,
Lyght as a lybard,
   Ther hym abyde the knyghtes.
He smote his schaft yn grate,
Almost hym thought* to late,
   Whanne he seygh hem wyth syghte ;
Lybeaus rood to hym thare,
Wyth a schaft all square,
   As man most of myghte.   1590

---

* Original reading : *Though.*

Eyther fmot other yn the scheld,
The peces fell ynto the feld,
  Of her schaftes schene ;
All tho that hyt beheld,
Ech man to other teld,
  The yonge knyghte ys kene.
Lambard was aschamed sore,
So nas he never yn feld before,
  To wyte and naght to wene ;
He cryde, Do come a stranger schaft,   1600
Yyf Artours knyght kan craft,
  Now hyt schall be sene.

Tho he tok a schaft rounde,
Wyth cornall scharp ygrounde,
  And ryde be ryght resoun ;
Ayder provede yn that stounde
To yeve other dedys wounde,
  Wyth fell herte as lyoun.
Lambard smot Lybeaus so
That hys scheld fell hym fro,   1610
  Into the feld adoun ;
So harde he hym hytte,
Unnethe that he myghte sytte
  Upryght yn hys arsoun.

Hys schaft brak wyth gret power,
Lybeaus hytte Lambard yn the launcer
  Of hys helm so bryght ;
That pysane, aventayle, and gorgere,
Fell ynto the felld fer,
  And syr Lambard upryght   1620
Sat, and rokkede yn hys sadell,
As chyld doth yn a kradell,
  Wythoute mannys myght ;
Ech man tok other be the hod,
And gonne for to herye good
  Borgays, baroun, and knyght.

Ayen to ryde Lambard thought,
Another helm hym was brought,
  And a schaft unmete ;

Whan they togydere mette,   1630
Ayder yn other scheld hytte,
 Strokes grymly greete.
Syr Lambardys schaft to-brast,
And syr Lybeaus sat so faste
 In sadelys as they setten,
That the styward, syr Lambard,
Fell of hys stede bakward,
 So harde they two metten.

Syr Lambard was aschamed sore,
Than seyde Lybeaus, Wyltow more?   1640
 And he answerede, Nay ;
Never seythe y was ybore,
Ne sygh ycome her before
 So redy a knyght to my pay.
A thoghth y have myn herte wythinne,
That thou art com of Gawenys kynne,
 That ys so stout and gay ;
Yef thou schalt for my lady fyght,
Well come to me, syr, thou knyght,
 In love and sykyr fay.   1650

Lybeaus answerede sykyrly,
Feyghte y schall for a lady,
 Be heste of kyng Artour ;
But y not wherfore ne why,
Ne who her doth swych vylany,
 Ne what ys her dolour.
A mayde, that ys her messengere,
And a dwerke me brought her,
 Her to do socour ; .
The constable seyde, Well founde   1660
Noble knyght of the table rounde,
 Iblessed be seynt Savour.

Anon that mayde Elene
Was fette wyth knyghtes ten,
 Before syr Lambard ;

Sche and the dwerk y mene
Tolde seven dedes kene,
   That he dede dydyrward;
And how that syr Lybeaus
Faught wyth fele schrewys,   1670
   And for no deth ne spared;
Lambard was glad and blythe,
And thonkede fele syde,
   God and seynt Edward.

Anon, wyth mylde chere,
They sete to the sopere,
   Wyth moch gle and game;
Lambard and Lybeaus, yn fere,
Of aventurs that ther wer,
   Talkede bothe yn same.   1680
Than seyde Lybeaus, syr Constable,
Tell me wythout fable,
   What ys the knyghtes name,
That halt so yn prisoune
The lady of Synadowne,
   That ys so gentyll a dame.

" Nay, syr, knyght ys he non,
Be god and be seynt Jon,
   That dorst away her lede;
Two clerkes beth her fon,   1690
Well fals of flessch and bon,
   That haveth ydo thys dede.
Hyt beth men of maystrye,
Clerkes of nygremansye,
   Hare artes for to rede;
Syr Maboun hatte that other,
And syr Irayn hys brother,
   For wham we beth yn drede.

Thys Yrayn and Maboun
Have imade of our toun   1700
   A palys queynte of gynne;
Ther nys knyght ne baroun,
Wyth herte harde as lyoun,
   That thorste come therinne.

Thys* ys be nygremauncye,
Ymaketh of fayrye,
  No man may hyt wynne ;
Therinne ys yn prysoun,
The lady of Synadowne,
  Ys come of knyghtes kynne.   1710

Ofte we hereth hyr crye,
But her to se wyth eye
  Therto have we no myghte ;
They doth her turmentrye,
And all vylanye,
  Be dayes and be nyght.
Thys Maboun and Irayn
Haveth swor deth certayn,
  To dethe they wyll her dyghte ;
But sche graunte hym tylle   1720
To do Mabounnys wylle,
  And yeve hem all her ryght.

Of alle thys dukdom feyr
That ylke ladyys eyr ;
  And come of knghtes kenne ;
Sche ys meke and boneyre,
Therfore we beth in despeyre,
  That sche be dyght to synne.
Than seyde Lybeaus desconus,
Be the grace of Jhesus,   1730
  That lady y schall wynne
Of Maboun and Yrayn ;
Schame i schall, certayne,
  Hem bothe wythout and wythinne.

Tho toke they har reste,
In lykynge as hem leste,
  In the castell that nyght ;

A morow Lybeaus hym prest
In armes that wer best
   And fressch he was to fyght.   1740
Lambard ladde hym forth well whate,
And broghte hym at the castell gate,
   And fond hyt open ryght,
No ferther ne dorste hym brynge,
For soth wythout lesynge,
   Erll, baroun, ne knyght.

But turnede hom agayn,
Save syr Gylet hys swayn
   Wolde wyth hym ryde ;
He swor his oth serteyn,   1750
He wold se hare brayn,
   Yf they hym wold abyde.
To the castell he rod
And hovede and abod,
   To Jhesu bad and tolde,
To sende hym tydynge glad
Of ham that longe had
   That lady yn prysoun holde.

Syr Lybeaus knyght certeys
Rod ynto the palys,   1760
   And at the halle alyghte ;
Trompes, schalmuses,
He seygh be for the hyegh deys
   Stonde yn hys syghte.
Amydde the halle flore
A fere stark and store
   Was lyght and brende bryght,
Nere the dore he yede,
And ladde yn hys stede,
   That wont was helpe hym yn fyght.   1770

Lybeauus inner gan pace,
To se ech a place,
   The hales yn the halle,
Of mayne mor ne lasse
Ne sawe he body ne face
   But menstrales yclodeth yn palle.

Wyth harp, fydele, and rote,
Orgenes, and mery note,
   Well mery they maden alle ;
Wyth sytole, and sawtrye,   1780
So moch melodye
   Was never wythinne walle.

Before ech menstrale stod
A torche fayre and good,
   Brennynge * fayre and bryght ;
Inner more he yode,†
To wyte wyth egre mode
   Ho scholde wyth hym fyghte.
He yede ynto the corneres,
And lokede on the pylers,   1790
   That selcouth wer of syghte,
Of jasper, and of fyn crystall,
Swych was pylers and wall,
   No rychere be ne myghte.

The thores wer of bras,
The wyndowes wer of glas,
   Florysseth wyth imagerye,
The halle ypaynted was,
No rychere never ther nas,
   That he hadde seye wyth eye.   1800
He sette hym an that deys,
The menstrales wer yn pes,
   That were go good and trye,
The torches that brende bryght
Quenchede anon ryght,
   The menstrales wer aweye.

Dores and wyndowes alle
Beten yn the halle,
   As hyt wer voys of thunder ;
The stones of the walle   1810
Over hym gon falle,
   That thought hym mych wonther.

---

* Original reading : *Brennyge.*
† Original reading : *Yede.*

That deys began to schake,
The erthe began to quake,
  As he satte hym under;
The rof abone unlek,
And the faunsere ek,
  As hyt wolde asonder.

As he sat thus dysmayde,
And held hymself betrayde,   1820
  Stedes herde he naye.
Thanne was he bette ypayd,
And to hymself he sayd,
  Yet y hope to playe.
He lokede ynto a feld,
Ther he sawe, wyth sper and scheld,
  Come ryde knytes tweye;
Of purpur Inde armure
Was lyngell and trappure,
  Wyth gold garlandys gay.   1830

That on rod ynto the halle,
And ther he gan to kalle,
  Syr knyght aunterous,
Swych cas ther ys befalle,
Thaugh thou be proud yn palle,
  Fyghte thou most wyth us.
Queynte thou art of gynne,
Yf thou that lady wynne,
  That ys so precyous.
Tho seyde Lybeaus, anon ryght,   1840
All fressch i am to fyght,
  Thorugh help of swete Jhesus.

Lybeaus wyth goodwyll
Into hys sadell gan skyll,
  And a launce yn hond he hent;
Quyk he rod hem tyll,
In feld hys son to fell,
  Therto was hys talent.
Togedere whan they mette
Upon har scheldes they sette   1850
  Strokes of thoughty dent:

Mabounys schaft to-brast,
Tho was he sore agast,
  And held hymself yschent.

And wyth that strok feloun
Lybeaus bar hym adoun
  Over hys horses tayle,
For hys hynder arsoun
To-brak and fyll adoun
  In that feld saunz fayle.   1860
And neygh he hadde hym sclayn,
Wyth that come ryde Yrayn
  Wyth helm, hauberke, and mayle,
All fressch he was to fyght,
He thought wyth mayn and myght
  Syr Lybeaus for to asayle.

Lybeaus of hym was war,
And sper to hym he bar,
  And lette hys brother stylle ;
Swych dent he smot dar   1870
That hys hauberke to-tar,
  And that lykede Yrayn ylle.
Har launces they brak atwo,
Swerdes they through out tho,
  Wyth herte grym and grylle,
And gonne for to fyghte,
Eyder prevede hys myghte
  Other for to spylle.

As they togedere hewe
Maboun the mare schrewe   1880
  In feld up aros ;
He sawe and well knew
That Yrayn smot dentys fewe,
  Therfore hym grym agros.
To Yrayn he ran ryght,
To helpe sle yn fyght
  Lybeaus that was of noble los ;
But Lybeaus faught wyth hem bothe,
Thaugh they wer never so wrothe,
  And kepte hymself yn clos.   1890

Whan Yrayn saw Maboun,
He smot a strok feloun
   To syr Lybeaus wyth yre,
Before [hys] forther arsoun
Als sket he karf adoun
   Of Lybeaus stede swyre.
But Lybeaus was werrour slegh,
And smot of hys theygh,
   Fell, and bone, and lyre ;
Tho halp hym naght hys armys   1900
Hys chauntement, ne hys charmys,
   Adoun fell that sory syre.

Lybeaus adoun lyght,
Afote for to fyghte,
   Maboun and he yn fere ;
Swych strokes they gon dyghte,
That sparkes sprong out bryght
   From scheld and helmes clerc.
As they togedere sette,
Har swerdes togedere mette,   1910
   As ye may lythe and lere ;
Maboun, that more schrewe,
To-karf that sworde of Lybeawe,
   A twynne quyt and skere.

Lybeaus was sore aschamed,
An yn hys herte agramede,
   For he hadde ylore hys sworde ;
And hys stede was lamed,
And he schulde be defamed,
   To Artour kyng, hys lord.   1920
To Yrayn tho he ran,
Hys sword he drough out than,
   Was scharp of egge, and ord ;
To Maboun he ran ryght,
Well faste he gan to fyght,
   Of love ther nas no word.

But ever faught Maboun,
As a wod lyoun,
   Lybeaus for the flo ;

But Lybeaus karf adoun 1930
Hys scheld wyth hys fachoun,
   That he tok Yrayn fro.
Wythout more tale teld,
The left arm wyth the scheld
   Well evene he smot of tho ;
Tho spak Maboun hym tylle,
Of thyne dentys ylle,
   Gentyll knyght, now ho.

And i woll yelde me,
In trewthe and lewtè, 1940
   At thyn owene wylle ;
And that lady fre,
That ys yn my poustè,
   I wyll the take tylle.
For thorugh that swordes dent
Myn hond y have yschent,
   That femyn wyll me spylle ;
I femynede hem bothe,
Sertayn wythoute nothe,
   In feld our fon to fylle. 1950

Seyde Lybeaus, Be my thryste,
I nell naght of thy yefte,
   All thys world to wynne ;
But ley on strokes swyfte,
Our on schall other lyste
   That hedde of be the skynne.
Maboun and Lybeaus
Faste togedere hewes,
   And stente for no synne ;
Lybeaus was more of myght, 1960
And karf hys helm bryght,
   And hys hedde atwynne.

Tho Maboun was ysclayn,
He ran ther he lefte Yrayn,
   Wyth fachoun yn hys fest ;
For to cleve hys brayn,
Therof he was certayn,
   And trewly was hys tryst.

And whanne he com thore,
Away he was ybore,   1970
   Whyderward he nyste ;
He softe hym for the nones,
Wyde yn alle the wones,
   To fyghte more hym lyste.

And whanne he ne fond hym noght,
He held hymself be caught,
   And gan to syke sare,
And seyde yn word and thought
Thys wyll be sore abought
   That he ys thus fram me yfare.   1980
On kne hym sette that gentyll knyght
And prayde to Marie bryght,
   Kevere hym of hys care ;
As he prayde thus yn halle
Out of the ston walle
   A wyndow doun fyll thare ;

And a greet wonder wythall
In hys herte gan fall,
   As he sat and beheld ;
A warm come out a pace,   1990
Wyth a womannes face,
   Was yong and nothyng eld.
Hyr body and hyr wyngys
Schynede yn all thynges,
   As gold gaylyche ygyld were,
Her tayle was myche unmete,
Hyr pawes grymly grete,
   As ye may lythe and lere.*

Lybeaus began to swete,
Ther he satte yn hys sete,   2000
   Maad as he were,
So sore hym gan agryse,
That he ne myghte aryse,
   Thaugh hyt hadde bene all afere.†

---

* This is the only stanza in which the poet has neglected the recurrent rhymes ;
in other respects it appears to be perfect.

† Conjectural emendation : *a fere.*

And er Lybeaus hyt wyste
The warm wyth mouth hym kyste,
   All aboute hys swyre ;
And after that kyssinge
The warmys tayle and wynge
   Anon hyt fell fro hyre.   2010

So fayr yn all thyng
Woman wythout lesyng
   Ne saw he never er tho,
But sche stod before hym naked,
And all her body quaked,
   Therfore was Lybeaus wo.
Sche seyde, Knyght gentyle,
God yelde the dy whyle,
   That my son thou woldest slo ?
Thou hast yslawe nouthe   2020
Two clerkes kouthe,
   To deeth they wold me have ydo.

Be est, north, and sowthe,
Be wordes of har mouthe,
   Well many man kouth they schend ;
Wyth hare chauntement,
To warm me hadde they ywent,
   In wo to welde and wende.
Tyll y hadde kyste Gaweyn,
Eyther som other knyght sertayn,   2030
   That wer of hys kende ;
And for thou savyst my lyf,
Casteles ten and fyf
   I yeve the wythouten ende :

And y to be thy wyf,
Ay wythouten stryf,
   Yyf hyt ys Artours wylle.
Lybeaus was glad and blythe,
And lepte to horse swythe,
   And lefte that ladye stylle.   2040
But ever he dradde Yrayn,
For he was naght yslayn,
   Wyth speche he wold hym spylle ;

To the castell gate he rode,
And hovede and abod,
   To Jhesu he bad wyth good wylle.

Sende hym tydyngys glad,
Of ham that long hadde
   That lady do vylanye ;
Lybeaus Lambard tolde,   2050
And othre knyghtes bolde,
   How hym there gan agye ;
And how Maboun was yslayn,
And wondede was Yrayn,
   Thorugh grace of seynt Marie ;
And how that lady bryght
To a warm was dyght,
   Thorugh kraft of chaunterye.

And how thrugh kus of a knyght
Woman sche was aplyght,   2060
   And a semyly creature ;
But sche stod me before,
Naked as sche was ybore,
   And seyde, now y am sure
My fomen beth yslayn,
Maboun and Yrayn,
   In pes now may we dure.
Whan syr Lybeaus, knyght of prys,
Hadde ytolde the styward, y wys,
   All thys aventure,   2070

A robe of purpure bys,
Ypelvryd wyth puryd grys,
   Anon he lette forth brynge ;
Calles and keverchefs ryche
He sent her pryvylyche,
   Anon wythout dwellynge ;
And whan sche was redy dyght,
Sche rod with mayn and myght,
   And wyth her another kyng ;
And all the peple of the toune,   2080
   Wyth a fayr processyoun,
   Thyder they gonne thrynge.

Whan the lady was come to towne,
Of gold and ryche stones a krowne,
   Upon her hedde was sette ;
And weren glad and blythe,
And thonkede god fele syde,
   That her bales bette.
All the lordes of dignytè,
Dede her omage and feawtè,   2090
   As hyt was due dette ;
Thus Lybeaus, wys and wyght,
Wan that ylke lady bryght,
   Out of the develes nette.

Sevè nyght they made sojour,
Wyth Lambard yn the tour,
   And all the peple yn same ;
And tho wente they wyth honour
To the noble kyng Artour,
   Wyth moche gle and game :   2100
And thonkede godes myghtes,
Artour and hys knyghtes,
   That he ne hadde no schame ;
Artour yaf her also blyve
Lybeaus to be hys wyfe,
   That was so gentyll a dame.

The joy of that bredale
Nys not told yn tale,
   Ne rekened yn no gest ;
Barons and lordynges fale   2110
Come to that semyly sale,
   And ladyes well honeste.
Ther was ryche servyse,
Of all that men kouth devyse,
   To lest and ek to mest ;
The menstrales, yn bour and halle,
Hadde ryche yftes wythalle,
   And they that weryn unwrest.

N

Fourty dayes they dwellde,*
And har feste helde,   2120
   Wyth Artour the kyng;
As the Frenssch tale teld,
Artour, wyth knyghtes beld,
   At hom gan hem brynge.
Fele yer they levede yn same,
Wyth moche gle and game,
   Lybeaus and that swete thyng.
Jhesu Cryst our savyour,
And hys moder, that swete flour,
   Graunte us alle good endynge.   2130

* Original reading : *dwelleds.*

www.ingramcontent.com/pod-product-compliance
Lightning Source LLC
Chambersburg PA
CBHW031443280326
41927CB00038B/1612